# Moments That Took My Breath Away

*I dedicate this story to my most beautiful and compassionate friend, wife Cindy; to my angelic daughter Beth who always cleared the most challenging pathway through life for me; to my darling daughter Katie, who arrived into this world with zeal and created more joys for me than I could ever count; and to my big-hearted son Joseph, who has created an extraordinary father-son relationship that represents hero to both him and me.*

# PROLOGUE

Life is not about the number of breaths we take but about the moments that take our breath away!

I'm 50 plus, and the number of moments that have taken my breath away are so monumental that I must share them now, in the prime of my life and at a time when I'm dying. I feel extraordinarily connected to every element of life - myself and what I'm living for, my wife, my children, my responsibilities as husband, my deep and abiding relationships with extended family and special friends, my commitment to job and community, and my belief in and abiding relationship with God.

I'm fully focused on what I'm going to leave behind in this life, and what I'm going to take with me from this life. Because of the disease I'm facing, I'm taking important moments every day to examine life deeply right now. And if I continue on this path, I'm confident my life will peak and I'll end up in an eternally euphoric paradise!

Feeling secure about life after five decades of living, I started making plans that leveled out the chaotic roller-coaster journey I'd lived up to. I was handling a challenging life so very well. I'd climbed a mountain, a steep one, with a child with grave needs, and I'd moved that monster. I was pretty confident I could take on anything else in life because nothing would be as significant, as monumental, as what I'd just handled for three decades.

During this rough-and-tumble journey, I clearly recognized that life is not about the number of breaths we take, despite the fact that I ran more than 40,000 miles in life and needed lots of deep breaths. Instead, life is about the moments that take our breath away!

As 2011 unfolded, I was a bit breathless, having been handed stunning and unsuspecting surprises that defined a life I never imagined living. But that was all behind me now and I was beginning to develop a new plan for the rest of my life.

I was running a PR firm, was executive director of a nonprofit disabilities foundation my wife and I had started in 1998, was president of the local YMCA Board of Directors, and was leading a movement in my community to improve health called Pioneering Healthier Communities. I was an elder at my church, and was overjoyed at the successes of my daughter Katie, who had just completed her degree at Ivy League Columbia University in Manhattan in occupational therapy, and my son Joseph, who was pitching at the Division I collegiate level at East Tennessee State University and was told by a major-league scout that he had MLB draft potential.

Phil plans, God laughs. Yes, He was stirring up something mighty different for me, a concoction of devastation, fear, fright, havoc, failure and grief. Or would it create something completely different in my life? Would I discover greater awe and wonderment in the depth of understanding of what life can give us in the face of devastation?

"Hey, fella! You aced round one of extraordinary trauma, overwhelming adversity, harrowing experiences, frightening diagnoses, and mind-numbing near-death adventures over a three-decade journey with your first-born daughter.

"Now, how about some icing on that cake?"

"What, who me? You talking to me?" I yelled back.

"How about a terminal illness. Can I make that your next calling?"

And without waiting for my answer, He handed me that proposition on a Monday morning in July in the year 2011.

"What, what ... whaaaaaaaat?"

Wait a big minute!

On 7-11-11, I learned that the 29 years I put my all into caring for a daughter who can't talk or walk, who has had thousands of grand mal seizures since she was three months old, who has a sleep disorder and a severe curvature of her spine, who has poor circulation in her pink, puffy feet, breathing dysfunctions, who can't swallow liquids, who has a feeding tube, a vagas nerve stimulator, osteoporosis, rosasia, and a diagnosis of Rett syndrome - all of this turned out to be a Ph.D. course and dissertation preparing me for a diagnosis of amyotrophic lateral sclerosis in the prime of my life.

At age 54, I was handed an ugly, insidious terminal illness that has no known cure. We'd obviously been pushed to our limits with Rett. Now I was given two to five years to live. ALS steals away all muscle strength until you can't walk, can't move, can't talk, can't swallow, can't breath, and can't live.

Here's the announcement: You've now had 30 years worth of blueprint work in handling a rare disorder in your first born child. So let's load you up with a motor neuron disorder. Can you handle Lou Gehrig's disease? It's something that's been around since 1869. No one has found a cure for this disease. It's time to ramp up your whole perspective on life to another gargantuan level or two or ten - or a trillion! You need more moments that will take your breath away, Phil Timp!

Day-by-day, moment-by-moment, my life has brought me to an understanding of what we can conquer if we grasp its significance, its power, its relevance, its purpose - even if that life is layered by pain, grief, sorrow, bewilderment, mystery. And even a stunning terminal illness.

I look at my life as privileged in many ways because it's been broken, then repaired, crushed, then recovered. Then crushed again. What lies ahead? Is that determined by how I take what I've learned and move that into a whole, new perspective?

Mine is an ordinary life in a lot of the routine aspects that frame our lives - it's a large-family childhood - seven kids and two medically-educated parents - followed by college, marriage to a high school sweetheart and the birth of three children. We raised our kids, moved a few times, changed jobs, stayed grounded, and loved each other with more intensity as the years went by.

Now, if I tell the stories within this bigger-picture story, well, that's where my story might differ pretty dramatically from yours; that's when you might define my story as extraordinary. It's been a climb up Mount Everest for three full decades. It's been a breathtaking adventure.

Deep into life, I've reached a unique understanding about the gift I was presented in the spring of 1982. When I accepted that gift, I began experiencing more than a quarter century of sobering, amazing, shocking, frightening and exhilarating highs and lows with a child who can't do anything for herself. However, it is this "child of nothing" who has transformed my world into one of everything that really matters!

She has made ordinary more than even extraordinary for me. Her kind of life has turned simple moments into profound memories for the scores of individuals - young and old - who have had the good fortune of crossing her path in their life's journey. And as I've witnessed all of this profundity, I've embraced every high and every low as notches in the circle of life that gets us to the finish line with arms raised triumphantly!

Through daughter Beth, I now know that in complete imperfection, there lies perfection in life. Let me explain - and give me some time to do so. Sit back and live it with me.

I'm going to require that you absorb it in large and small doses of hurt and happiness because that's the only way I will allow it to unfold. After all, it's the way wife Cindy and I experienced it. A little bit of joy, then a whole lot of hurt, then a little more hurt followed by profound - and surprising - joy. Breath, no breath. Back and forth, up and down, high and low, dark then bright, then brighter, then the ultimate celebration of joy!

Look what we got in life, I boast now! A mysterious curiosity, an angel *and* a saint. A silent bombshell of a child who doesn't let us sit back and drift along in life but rather one who forces profundity on us at every turn. It has made, for me, a life of extraordinary satisfaction. It has made life complete. And it prepared me for much more.

"Here I am," Beth's life shouts to us. "Do something great with me. Make me. Mold me. Fill me. Use me."

Okay. Here we go.

# The Year Is 1980

Two years before our daughter arrived and our lives were changed forever, I decided to join tens of thousands of people across America in what was then called "the running boom." The year was 1980, the day was January 4, and distance running became way more than a hobby for Phil Timp. It evolved into a severe addiction of endorphin highs!

I wanted good health for a long time because my dad wasn't with us any longer because of poor health. If I got his bad heart genes, I wanted to build my heart stronger so that I wouldn't experience what he did way too early in life.

Time on the road, pounding the pavement, also gave me time to mull things through in my mind, like writing assignments at the newspaper, how our family budget was holding together with two $10,000 jobs, and when we would head home to the mountains of Southwest Virginia again and enjoy wild times at "the farm" with my brothers-in-law.

I also had a very competitive nature regarding this whole running thing, targeting the marathon, a 26.2-mile monster as my eventual goal.

Problem is, I set that marathon goal a mere two months after I started running any distance at all.

And so in mid-March, I stood at the starting line of the Shamrock Marathon in Virginia Beach, downright confident that I could conquer this distance in under four hours, even though my longest training run had been only 17 miles. I wasn't aware of "the wall" until I hit it at mile 18 on the Boardwalk along the Atlantic

Ocean coastline. Stupid me, I had not taken a single drop of water along the way to hydrate my body.

My struggles escalated significantly. My hamstrings were screaming in pain. I stopped to walk, but that hurt worse than trying to continue jogging. I stretched and screamed in greater pain. I hit the park at mile 21, and a 70 year old, white-haired gentleman - and I mean gentle man - pulled up alongside me, put his arm around me and asked me what my finishing time goal was.

"Four hours, I've gotta go under four hours," I sputtered. Little was left in me.

"You've still got time," he said. He was walking with me. "Let's go this together. Let's get back into a rhythm."

And so I did. I cleared that hurdle. A mile later, this kind man picked up his pace and eased out ahead of me as my struggles intensified. "You can get there," he said. Then he was gone.

Time was ticking away and I pushed myself to keep the slow jog going. I got a boost at mile 23 when a runner passed me with a friend riding a single-speed bicycle next to him. The bike had an old-fashioned basket on the front and a huge boom box, the early version of the iPod, sitting on that basket, was blasting the Rolling Stones' "Jumpin' Jack Flash." The song swirled in my mind as a motivator long after the runner and his friend disappeared out ahead of me.

I worked my way through mile 24 and mile 25. With 1.2 miles remaining, the crowd along the street heading back into downtown Virginia Beach was growing. I spotted two women cheering us on, and on the street in front of them was a carton of orange juice. I needed sustenance badly, and walked to them.

"That's your orange juice?" I asked. "And if so, could I have it?"

"Oh, yes!" They were both overjoyed that they could help me in a desperate moment.

And down it went, every drop, within seconds. The lactic acid buildup in my calves, hamstrings and quadriceps was overwhelmingly painful. But I had new life in my belly and a real desire in my heart to close this marathon out.

I thanked the women for their kindness and turned to get back on course. Running by me was an Asian woman with a short stride. I jumped in behind her and developed a strategy that would get me to the finish line. When she puts her right foot down, you do the same, Phil Timp. Left foot, left foot. Right, left, right left.

The crowd built. And I saw Cindy's proud grin. Her voice gave me that extra push to crash across the finish line. And crash I did! I fell on a patch of grass, totally spent but exhilarated that I finished in 3 hours, 56 minutes!

I learned a lot about the body during that trying experience. It was a brutal experience; was it something I'd want to even try again? I was a mess during that March marathon and for days after. I had to walk backwards down any set of stairs because my quads were so beaten up!

I recognized that I needed to feed and water my 6'2" and 155 pound body way more effectively during any race. And I realized that I could run this distance much faster if I worked smarter in my training. So, yes, I was a confirmed marathoner with the goal of creating PRs every time I toed the starting line.

I began running more miles and began mixing speed into those miles that spring and summer. Then I put my application in to run the Marine Corps Marathon in Washington, D.C., in November.

The cannon boom made me jump at the starting line in D.C. and it kicked up my adrenaline. Those first three miles were challenging because slower runners were out ahead of me and I had to avoid tripping over them. We circled a full mile around the Pentagon and headed toward the monuments. My pace was smooth, easy - and fast. I hydrated at every stop, grabbing a paper cup filled with water and pouring half of it on my head and then pinching the cup for a spout that would allow me to both drink and keep my pace up.

East Potomac Park at Hains Point near the main branch of the Potomac River was the toughest stretch for all of us runners. The crowds were slim to none; it was a place in the race - miles 17, 18 and 19 - where "the wall" can rise up suddenly I struggled through it, but kept up my sub-7 minute per mile pace.

The last 10K was a mental mountain to climb; I had to push my legs and arms from my brain. I was no longer on automatic pilot. I passed runners and runners passed me. I was alternately surging, then slipping back.

Then came the Iwo Jima Memorial half-mile hill to the finish line. Those Marine Corps soldiers hoisting that American flag gave me the momentum I needed to surge across that finish line in 2 hours, 59 minutes and a few seconds. I broke 3 hours!

Better yet, I knocked 57 minutes off my marathon time in a mere eight months! I dropped my average per mile pace from 9 minutes in March to 6 minutes and 52 seconds in November.

I was a Boston Marathon qualifier! In the running world, that was the ultimate gold medal! Yes, that was breathtaking!

## The Year Is 1982

Much anticipated, much bally-hooed! At precisely 4:50 on the afternoon of May 25, 1982, at Riverside Hospital in Newport News, Virginia, life became an exclamation mark for us!

That's when baby Beth was born. Elizabeth Nicole Timp, more accurately stated.

She was mostly understated, arriving a month late at six pounds and 11 ounces and emitting not even a whimper when she arrived into this world. She didn't cry - but we did because in less than 24 hours after her arrival, she'd make a huge statement about what life would be like for her - and for us - forever!

For the vast majority of parents, life for their newborn evolves second by second, moment by moment. That precious newborn will sleep, pee, poop, open eyes, cry, suck on fingers and then repeat those basic, essential practices. Those are the highlights that a newborn exhibits, and every parent is simply amazed at witnessing each of these "exclamation mark" moments! And as the days roll by, the obvious developmental aspects of most children continue to evolve in a predictable pattern.

Then there's Beth.

I began replacing the period with the exclamation mark in all aspects of my communication after baby Beth was born. And I haven't slowed down. For me, that exclamation mark defines life! Every moment - like every sentence, if it's worth writing - needs a strong closing, an attention-grabber, and a slam-the-door kind of statement!

Life needs to be lived wide-open, determined, non-stop, full speed! Didn't always know that - but I kicked life in high gear when Beth showed up!

Without that optimistic outlook, this book wouldn't be written. Without that philosophy, I wouldn't have traveled very far at all down this road of ruts and bumps in life. When the frightening fork in the road rose up in front of Cindy and me, we wouldn't have picked the right path without our exclamation mark pushing us in the right direction. Without that can-do attitude, the child my wife and I were given to raise wouldn't be the victorious achiever she has become in life!

---

I don't know of a woman who wanted to be a mom more than my wife. And when a pregnancy is close to perfect, as Cindy's was, your birthing expectations are off the charts. Things will go better than great. I was at her side after attending every birthing class. We were ready!

For starters, we had to wait, almost a month beyond the due date of May 1, 1982, my 25th birthday. Things were happening but this was child number one and things don't always happen on time with child number one.

Cindy defined herself as tough, refusing to even ask about an epidural, let alone request one when the pain - and labor itself - slowed to a crawl hours into the process. When she pushed, she broke more blood vessels on her face, which spoke to the pain she was enduring. Labor was truly labor redefined. But the determination in Cindy's eyes screamed the message "I *will* win this fight."

So stoic Cindy pushed on, until the moment arrived when she needed a lot more from gravity to help her baby girl arrive into this world. Our nurse moved her carefully to a new room and a birthing chair that allowed her to grab handles and force our newborn out into this world.

Elizabeth Nicole Timp was spanked like every other newborn, but she cried not at all. We wanted to hear that wail, that moment when that enormous breath of life was taken by our firstborn child, a sign that she was alive and well. And I mean well.

Silence. No scream. No cry. Silence.

Little did we know or expect or anticipate that silence would be the trademark of our daughter's life.

Why wasn't she crying? There was no answer. The obstetrician was more concerned with her tiny feet, which were folded up toward the outside of her legs in a very odd position. Within the next 48 hours, we would learn from an orthopedic surgeon that the navicular and talis bones in both of our daughter's feet were in the wrong place. It was a condition called bilateral vertical talis, and we had no clue that this would be the first of many unforgiving health issues our infant daughter would face in life.

The pregnancy was perfect; everything that would follow after birth would be so imperfect. Beth didn't rock and roll in the womb like she should have, but we didn't know she should have because this was our first-born child. This nine-month pregnancy, as serene and comfortable as any could be, would evolve into a lifetime of trauma for a mother who deserved none of this.

But we would find out very quickly that life - and all of its circumstances - are not about what you deserve. We all have certain expectations that should be carried out in full. And, of course, you need to have expectations in life. Otherwise, you won't accomplish anything. But broken feet at birth? What was that about?

---

Will she stand? Will she walk? I can't answer that question, the orthopedic doctor tells us.

If it comes down to our commitment, to our level of dedication and devotion to making sure our daughter can walk, there won't be any hesitation on our part. We are high achievers. Have always been. Cindy and I did everything we could to excel in high school and in college. I played for the winningest high school baseball coach in Virginia history. I ran the two-mile in the state track meet. I was the MVP on our basketball team and was the number 1 seed on our tennis team. Cindy and I won awards on stage as actors and as forensics state champions. Cindy was the top student in her class at Virginia Tech, a summa cum laude graduate. I grabbed a cum laude degree from Washington & Lee University as a journalism major. I wanted to repeat what Bob Woodward and Carl Bernstein did when they uncovered the Watergate scandal under Richard Nixon in the 1970s. Investigative reporting? Yes, my specialty. My dream!

Could we help Beth stand and walk? You betcha!

A.I. DuPont Institute in Wilmington, Delaware, would try to help us turn life - and Beth's feet - in the right direction when Beth was seven months of age. This orthopedic hospital and its exceptional surgical staff would put the navicular and talis bones in the right place in Beth's feet, first the right foot, then the left foot. To prepare for this surgical work, her feet would have to be casted for weeks to stretch the skin. It would take me hours to soak the casts off her feet - time and time again - as she laid in my lap - again in complete silence. She was teaching us patience as parents, a virtue we would be asked to practice countless times throughout the course of life with this child.

Would this surgery give our daughter the chance to ever stand and walk in life? We were told that chance would be limited. If there was any chance at all, this young couple would push way beyond the possibility of this happening and move to a level of probability.

However, long before we would make our first trip to Wilmington, our life with Beth blew up on us unexpectedly when she was only three months of age. At a family gathering, her uncle Jeff, the youngest of Cindy's five brothers, was cradling Beth in his arms when he suddenly noticed her eyes widening and locking in place. Her body stiffened, and he shouted out to us that something serious was wrong with Beth.

The diagnosis was epilepsy. Beth had experienced the first of thousands of grand mal seizures in her life. Phenobarbital was the first of more than a dozen seizure medications we would attempt to use to try to control these horrific, life-changing episodes in our daughter's life. They would clearly rob her of her quality of life for days and sometimes weeks at a time. They would erupt during the night, and we learned that we had to sleep with a monitor by our bedside in order to hear Beth gasp when the seizure would begin. If we didn't hear the start of even a single seizure, there could be the chance that she wouldn't breath through the seizure because her air passage might be blocked by the position of her head after the convulsions occurred.

Through the course of my life, that monitor clearly became the lifeline between us and our daughter's seizure disorder. I became the light sleeper, and because Beth developed a poor sleep pattern, waking up during the course of the night to hum herself back to sleep for hours at a time, my nights became largely sleep deprived.

To save my daughter's life, I was willing to lean into that bedside monitor - and say no to REM sleep - to make sure that what I was listening to was a gentle, peaceful sound coming from my angel daughter - and not the frightening, rhythmic sound of her body violently shaking for up to a minute while in a state of unconsciousness, the result of yet another grand mal seizure. The sprint to Beth's room took only seconds, and we were by her side to witness another frightening out-of-body experience and help her breathe through this five-minute crisis time and again.

And so here we are, three months into life with our firstborn and she is already bent and broken physiologically and neurologically. How do we move forward? I had no real answer, other than to take on each day moment by moment and hope that we could get to tomorrow. Way too often, Cindy and I would sink into a corner of a room in our house along the Chesapeake Bay in Hampton, Virginia, and cry together, not sure we could arrive at any tomorrow!

The cycle of disruption continued at a doctor's visit when Beth was six months old. The standard measuring tests showed that the growth of Beth's head had slowed down and had actually fallen off the growth chart. We were hearing the word "microcephalic" time and again, even though Beth was experiencing limited growth throughout her entire person. To her mom and I, she was just small all over. But we couldn't ignore the medical reports that showed significant slowing down of her head circumference. And we were well aware that a small head can mean a small brain, which can mean developmental delays and the real possibility of intellectual disabilities.

Was that why she was also not reaching milestones in her ability to roll over and sit up at six months of age? Her muscle strength seems to be limited. She was soft. She was weak. All in all, Beth looked like she was slipping completely off the chart of "normal."

Cindy and I questioned how we could possibly get through the dual surgeries on Beth's feet before all these other significant issues had emerged. Would we survive the trip to Delaware with a child who was falling apart before our very eyes?

That small head, what did that mean, for the present and future for our baby girl? Small head, small brain, mental retardation?

Was this confirmed? No. Was this suffocating us with pain and agony? Absolutely! Life had steered way off course for Phil and Cindy. At age 25, we wondered what we'd done wrong to deserve a rocky terrain in our brand new travels as parents.

We didn't know what to expect because our daughter at six months, like any child who just arrived into this world, wasn't able to be "tested" for her cognitive ability.

Over time, we noticed that Beth's hands began coming together and wouldn't come apart, unless we separated them for her. Those hands were busy, almost frantic, but Beth herself didn't appear to be troubled by this strange anomaly. She worked her hands with a steady smile on her face. It had to feel good to her.

The medical teams we were engaged with couldn't answer our questions. They had no awareness of this mix of oddities affecting our daughter and didn't know if they were syndromatic.

Instead, they labeled Beth with a mild case of cerebral palsy. With a smaller than normal head, she was microcephalic, too. Or maybe she was just developmentally delayed, without a direct diagnosis. In any regard, we had no real answer about this unusual combination of disabilities.

Mother Cindy and daughter Beth are wrapped in love.

## The Year Is 1983

The first couple of years of Beth's life were filled with oddities and even a few memorable milestones. She breast fed well from the beginning of her life and began eating solid foods at six months of age. At 10 months old, Beth was able to hold a cup with both hands and drink from it.

It was obvious she recognized Cindy and me at age 4 months. At 5 1/2 months, she was sitting up by herself, and at 10 months, she began crawling with a little help. Halfway through her first year, Beth began making some vocal sounds that mirrored the sounds that her cousins of the same age were making, which had us excited and hopeful! At seven months of age, Beth said her first - and only - word, which was "mama" and she said it with every ounce of purpose and meaning toward her own mother. However, we would later learn through neurological tests that the grand mal seizures were occurring in the speech center of Beth's brain, wiping clean her ability to pronounce words.

Meanwhile, we were inspired by all that was transpiring from a child we felt would have a limited IQ. There were some quirks in her behavior that puzzled us. She would giggle at strange noises around her and had a fascination for sharp designs, letters and numbers. She would stare intently at logos on shirts. She became enamored by the print in books and magazines to the point where she would race across a room on her knees if she spotted a book to grab it and begin pulling the pages apart. Her hands were in constant motion; when she didn't have them together, wringing them vigorously, she had a book or magazine in them working it with everything in her to "pull its contents out."

Beth never cried much and babies cry a lot! She had powerfully strong legs but very weak shoulders. She had an unusual sleep habit of grasping her hands together. I called it a prayerful pose, one she has expressed all 30 years of her life! And she tended to pay attention to people way more than any toy or animal around her.

At 16 months of age, Beth was knee walking quite well and she could sit Indian style and pull her socks off her feet by herself, an impressive milestone and one that stood out to her mother and me.

By year 2, Beth was even feeding herself with her own fork after we pierced the food on her plate for her. And it was clear by that second year that she was left-handed. By age 3, she began cruising around furniture on her tiny feet, the miraculous result of successful foot surgery, and our dream of her walking on her own was growing even closer to reality! Soon, she was sliding off her bed and the couch by herself and even climbing up on both, skills of dexterity we simply didn't expect from our disabled daughter. Was she establishing the blueprint for fight, despite the mountains she had to climb in life?

We looked at preschool opportunities, firmly believing that early intervention with a child with multiple anomalies and no diagnosis would benefit our Beth greatly! By age 3 and weighing in at only 22 pounds, she was attending Rhea Valley Elementary School in rural Virginia. Her ride to school was shared by a youngster named Jeremy, who reached out to hold Beth's hand in the back seat of the car.

It was clear that Beth was having an early impact on the lives of everyone with whom she ever came in contact!

As 1983 rolled along, I was knocking my marathon times down race after race. I was adding to my weekly mileage, jumping from 60 a week to 85 miles per week. I was sacrificing sleep to get faster. I was relieving the stress in a world of mysteries and medical uncertainties involving our dear Beth by racing hard and finishing in the top 1% of any race I ran.

I had knocked out a 16:05 5K (5:10 per mile pace) and a 33:40 10K (5:25 per mile). I was training hard at shorter distances but was targeting a marathon for the coming year. I ran a 1 hour, 15 minute, 30 second half-marathon in Parkersburg, West Virginia. I raced with Janis Klecker, the women's winner, to accomplish that fast time, a pace of 5:43 per mile!

But one of the biggest running highlights of my entire life didn't have anything to do with me officially racing. It came down to helping my oldest brother-in-law, Marty Prince, establish a fast enough pace at the Marine Corps Marathon to qualify for the Boston Marathon.

Marty has a level of determination in accomplishing a goal - even it takes him to his last breath of life! And this race just about reached that moment! Today, he is one of East Tennessee's best pulmonologists. He's also got a passion for music as a lifetime singer, songwriter and guitar player. His own band, called Remedy, is made up of physicians who enjoy their leisure time playing music.

Back in the '80s, Marty told me I inspired him to run. His words meant so much to me:

"I will simply explain how you changed my whole life. I was a struggling medical student and pretty much a physical wreck. Sure, I had once been a high school footballer and weight room freak, but more than half a decade of constant studying and consumption of at least 3 large pizzas a week resulted in a plump, unconditioned 25 year old.

"Around this time, you took up the strange and exotic habit of actually running for fun and physical fitness. Initially I thought you had lost it, Bozo, but soon I found myself thinking if you could do it, why not me? My initial half-mile jog/walk around the MCV campus proved to be a near fatal event, but it convinced me that something had to change and that perhaps you, my insane brother in law, were not as deranged as I had previously thought.

"Over the final few months of my senior year in medical school, running became a pretty big deal. I worked my way up to the 10K distance, and we shared a few family 10K runs before Jacque and I set off to Dallas for my internship. I thought I was doing pretty well; a genuine running machine but then I got word that you had gone and run a marathon! Now I am not saying that we were ever competitive, but I can distinctly recall that the day I heard about your marathon was the day I signed up for the Dallas White Rock Marathon. The fact that the marathon was only eight weeks away did not seem to be much of a problem. I thought, hey, Phil did it, so why not me? After completing the White Rock and nearly winding up in the ICU with renal failure, it finally occurred to me that you were actually something I was not - a truly gifted endurance athlete. I was humbled but strangely inspired to continue.

"So despite my difficult start as a marathoner, you are nothing but encouraging. One race led to another over the next couple of years. Jacque and I wound up in Chapel Hill and I found myself lined up for the 1983 Marine Corps Marathon in Washington D.C.

"You had not been marathon training that fall but to my delight and surprise, you insisted on being there to pace and encourage me. It turns out you were the key to the most important athletic achievement of my life that day. You didn't just jog a few miles to provide moral support. You ran mile after mile with me. Five, 10, 15 and finally 20 long miles!

"The whole way you coached and encouraged me. You slowed me down when I was trying to run 5:30 miles and pushed me through a couple of fading spells. When you finally dropped off at 20 miles, I knew I was going to have a pretty good time. But you are not done with me yet; you knew I wanted to qualify for the Boston Marathon and had to run a sub-2 hour and 50 minute race.

"As I neared the final half-mile uphill to the finish line at the Iwo Jima Memorial, I began to fade badly. I did not think I could find the strength to sprint that last uphill stretch to qualify. But before I could give up, you were there running along the edge of the crowd screaming at me like a madman!

"You had me charging up that hill and across the finish line with a whole second to spare!

"To this day, I still don't know how you got from Hains Point back to the finish before I did. I do know that without your inspiration and encouragement, I would have never run a single 10K, let alone competitive marathons.

"I became a lifelong endurance athlete because of your passion and enthusiasm. My life was truly transformed because of your example. Thank you, my brother!"

After collapsing on the grass and catching his breath, Marty picked himself up and I threw my arms around him in victory! Today, Marty can no longer run without threatening an injury, so he has transferred his passion for aerobic exercise to two wheels. Closing in on 60 soon, he remains one hell of an endurance athlete!

## The Year Is 1986

Looking at Beth as a burden rather than a bountiful blessing was a massive weight on my heart as we headed to Charlottesville, Virginia, during Easter week of 1986 for a one-week evaluation at the Children's Rehabilitation Center. We were told we'd get answers about her future, good or bad. Doctors, therapists and educators were going to evaluate Beth over the course of a week to determine that future.

Cindy and I had not yet reached our 30s, and we didn't know what kind of testing the experts in Charlottesville would throw at our daughter in order to give us an IQ and some idea of what her potential productivity might be as she moved ahead in life.

Beth was two months shy of her fourth birthday. She was a waif of a child at 30 pounds. She wore a big smile most of the time, couldn't speak a word, and had her hands locked together. Beth was such a curiosity for us at this time in her life. When she saw something she wanted, those little hands would come apart instantaneously and she would tear into her motivational desire. However, if you threw a command at her, she had no interest in following it. Or maybe she was just one stubborn young lady.

It was time to test those commands at the rehab facility in March of 1986. On day one of our visit, a therapist would run Beth through a set of standardized tests, not knowing what her strange combination of anomalies were all about. She sat Beth down Indian style in front of her and placed a block and a bucket in front of our daughter. Her request was simple and direct: Beth, please pick up that block and put it in the bucket.

Our daughter looked at the therapist, then looked down at the block and bucket and began leaning forward toward those objects. She began rocking back and forth, and a smile crossed her face. And she rocked harder.

But she didn't separate her hands and she didn't speak words of wisdom because she couldn't. The therapist encouraged her repeatedly, but our little girl wasn't getting it done.

And so she "failed" that test. And others throughout the week. In fact, it took only three days for the team of evaluators to determine that our daughter didn't really have much "upstairs" because she couldn't speak or separate her hands to follow commands.

Cindy and I witnessed this crushing reality, standardized test after standardized test. We were discouraged with each passing moment, but Beth wasn't. She was trapped but she wasn't frustrated. She smiled her way through the week, showing everyone around her that she was a determined little angel who just couldn't perform the tests they threw at her.

Then Holy Thursday arrived. The 8th of May. Enough tests, more than enough failure. The medical staff lined up a meeting that afternoon to discuss "results." What did the future hold for Beth? That was their objective for the week, but I'm pretty sure we could have held the meeting by ourselves, delivered the grim news to ourselves, and left with the same sad story they shared with us that day.

"Your daughter is severely mentally disabled with an IQ of 25."

It was our "death sentence," delivered from a kind, compassionate medical team.

But she smiles, she recognizes mom and dad, she loves to look at letters and numbers and designs of all kind. There's got to be something there! Surely it's just hidden by the fact that she can't speak and use her hands effectively. Right?

---

I picked a slumping Cindy up from her chair as we graciously thanked the team of experts there at the Children's Rehabilitation Center.

And then, leaning hard on each other, we took the longest, loneliest walk of our lives down that sterile white hallway to our room. Our emptiness was extreme. The crown of thorns was penetrating. Our hope was battered back to nothing.

Our room felt like a prison cell. We were given a life sentence of grief, sorrow and pain, as we would witness little to nothing from our daughter.

I wanted to say something positive to my broken wife about how we were going to rise up and conquer this desperation; that our waif angel was not gone for good; that we'd find a sliver of spirit that we'd resurrect into something that would grow and become greatness for her! But there was nothing there at that time.

A wordless walk is all we had left in us.

We lovingly dressed Beth in her PJs and collapsed into each other's arms, the hurt overflowing from our eyes, staining faces that had - up to now - held undeniable determination that we'd move past all this disruption and find a daughter who was like all others in action and appearance.

Cindy's pain was overtaken by exhaustion and she fell deep asleep in my arms. I didn't fall asleep. I didn't know what to do or who to talk to. Dial up loving parents and I'd evaporate into yet another pool of tears and create a panic on the other end.

The emptiness we encountered that night felt like the final step into the dungeon of hell. My soul had flamed out; I had nothing left. And neither did Cindy.

Was this a child we needed? What would she give us in life? Would she rob us of our professional dreams because we would have to focus so much of our daily living on her? She wouldn't reach milestones of a high school graduation, college, dating and eventually a wedding, her own children, our grandchildren!

These devastating thoughts swirled through my mind throughout the night and into Good Friday. I couldn't share them with Cindy, but I knew the limited lifetime highlights in Beth's life would be few and far between and would be nothing we could anticipate. And I knew my wife was focusing on that downward spiral.

Dawn did not awaken me that Good Friday morning. When it arrived, I had already laced up my Asics running shoes and pushed through the front doors of the rehab center for an opportunity to change my perspective on life on some two-lane back road highway in Charlottesville. I was determined to put in a 10-mile training run to relieve a little stress and find a way to endure at least one more day of heartache and pain.

At age 29, I was in the prime of my distance running career. A 10-mile run was easy under normal circumstances. Often, this kind of run would be sprinkled with what we runners called fartleks - or fast interval half-mile and mile sprints well under six minutes per mile. Pushing through the pain of those kinds of workouts allowed me to maintain a very fast pace in achieving two-hour and forty minute marathons in places like Chicago and Washington, D.C.

This Friday morning run was flavored much differently. The pain was in my heart, not in the lactic acid buildup in my muscles. I couldn't run hard or fast today. I was paying close attention to what was surrounding me, the beauty of the Blue Ridge Mountains in the distance as I climbed hills and powered down the other side of this rolling terrain, early morning mist drifting off the Rivanna River, creating a fresh feeling in a set of lungs that needed some new life, a breath of new hope!

Absorbing a sense of renewed energy cleared my clouded mind and led me to an ethereal place that brought prayer to my heart. A determination unlike anything I had ever experienced came to me, pushing me to go one-on-one with God. I opened up with both barrels aimed at my Heavenly Father.

"This challenge is overwhelming me!" I screamed from my heart. "What have You handed my wife and me? Where are You when we need You most? God, what are You requiring of us? Why do we have to be the couple that must endure unlimited and unending pain? Did we really deserve this? I can't do this. Cindy can't do this. Our army of support can't fight through this and resolve it.

"Give me an answer, and give it to me now!"

I broke down and began to cry so deeply that I couldn't breathe and had to stop running for the first time ever during a training run. And then I realized that the intensity of by prayer was being addressed, right then and there.

Trust Me. Do you trust Me? If you do, you will walk away from the edge of the cliff and take that path of serenity instead. You will allow Me to hold your hand as we begin to ascend the mountain. Allow Me to intervene in your every waking moment of living. In doing so, you will view your angel daughter as a bountiful blessing, and life will be rich and rewarding for you and your special family forever.

That sensation of peace and tranquility filled me to overflowing. Yes, I said to God's request. I can do that. I *will* do that. And I did.

I arrived back at the rehab center with fresh legs and a completely refreshed spirit. It was time to share this breathless moment with Cindy. It was time for both of us to escape from Alcatraz and head to paradise!

---

I didn't wake my wife up as I gently opened the door to our room. It was still early in the morning, and Cindy had finally fallen asleep in the early morning hours of Good Friday.

I opened my briefcase and grabbed a pad of paper. Where do I begin to share our journey of hope that lies ahead? I broke into tears, and then began writing. Wrong words. I can do better, I can be stronger. And I began to cry again. I wanted to get this right; everything was at stake - hope for stronger living and insight into what stronger living will lead to in the end. "Give it to me, Lord," I prayed.

And the words came to me:

*Dear Cindy,*

*I've started this letter four times but the pages keep filing up with tears. This is Good Friday, a day Christ suffered and died for you and me. I'll bet he cried along the road as he carried that heavy cross, afraid of his impending death.*

I wish he were here today. I'd find him and invite him to our home and ask him to touch Beth and make her well. I'll bet he'd think she was a pretty special little girl, too.

You know we've got a huge challenge ahead of us, you and me - together. This is our cross to shoulder – and yet we've got someone who's willing to help share the burden – if we let Him.

Easter Sunday is only two days away, and I can somehow clearly focus on Christ's resurrection into heaven and how much that means to all of us.

We'll have our day with Beth, Cindy. We'll join her in God's kingdom. You can rest assured she's already got a little chair carved out for her next to God's right hand. She'll be there with Christopher, and Mathew and Scottie ... and all the other little kids we've met here this week. She'll wait for us to arrive – and then she'll run into our arms – that beautiful smile lighting up her angelic face.

There in heaven we will find peace at last ... the reward will be ours. God will welcome us home.

Love,

Phil

We talked, hugged, kissed, packed our bags and headed back home to the Appalachian Mountains. And life became rich and rewarding!

This couple climbed mountains and then moved them in the course of their 34 years of marriage.

On September 28 of 1986, Cindy and I headed across the street in our Bristol, Virginia, neighborhood to visit one of Cindy's five brothers, Bill, and his wife, Gena. Cindy and I shared many moments with this couple, most of them medical surprises that were poignantly gripping. As we broke, they were part of the family that continuously tried piecing us back together. Bill was emerging as the leader of a construction company that would eventually win the bids on standout corporate, education, arts and religious landmark projects that gave new life to the region's landscape. Wife Gena, a former teacher, shared her husband's drive to make a significant difference in the lives of others. In her case, it was all about helping women struggling with self-esteem issues. Her role was senior director in the Mary Kay world and she impacted hundreds of lives playing this role.

Beth was all of 4 years, 4 months and 3 days old, and we still had no diagnosis of her overall condition. Thus, she continued being quite a mystery to us, almost on a daily basis. And on this Sunday afternoon, she was ready to surprise us with a miracle moment!

She was so petite at the time, not quite 30 pounds, and we didn't know why she couldn't gain weight. We did know that she wasn't walking on her own yet and we weren't sure she ever would.

Until that afternoon when she revived a dream in us that we'd created on day two of her life!

I had Beth in my arms in the kitchen. We were making small talk with Bill and Gena, catching up on the week's activities when I got a bold idea and decided to see how secure Beth might be on her little feet.

So I gently placed her on the floor in a standing position. The green and white patterned tile is a surface I'll always remember. It wound up being a dream field for us all!

With no hesitation whatsoever, our waif of an angel just flat took off on her own! Step one, then two. I reached out to help balance her but she was already into steps three and four, and then five.

The miracle unfolded right then and there. The noise - the celebratory cheer - grew louder with each step.

Her little gait was a waddle. Steps six and seven and then eight! And then she stopped on a dime, her tiny hands clasped tightly. And all four of us - mom, dad, uncle and aunt - rushed to her side to grab her, swoop her up in our collective arms and shout to the heavens!

Our angel had pulled it off and it was time to celebrate with hugs and tears and phone calls to family members far and wide!

That was an early miracle - and there might be more!

Phil expresses his sincere love to daughter Beth.

## The Year Is 1988

Running was keeping me alive in the face of some steep mountains that kept rising before us. The endorphin highs that I reached in my every day training helped me not only survive but also actually thrive. I was addicted to running, running fast, and racing. My success on the roads gave me confidence that I could take on anything at home.

Bill Rodgers and Alberto Salazar were America's fastest marathoners in the 1980s. I couldn't emulate their speed, but I could match their desire. In doing so, I happened to team up with a training partner who surprised me with her unexpected talent.

Teresa Ornduff, a golfer in high school who didn't take up running until after her college days to just stay in shape, was a complete surprise in the running world. We both lived in Abingdon, Virginia, which gave us the opportunity to meet on the street at 4:30 in the morning to tackle our training runs. I was impressed with Teresa's emerging talent as a runner because she had an unorthodox, choppy stride that definitely did not look world-class. But she had an oxygen uptake that rivaled that of Joan Benoit Samuelson, the first ever women's winner of an Olympic marathon in 1984.

As Teresa and I began ramping up our weekly mileage, her 10K times began dropping from the high 30s to the mid-30s. She began winning large regional races, and we began hitting the track for intense workouts that gave us both faster leg turnover and faster finishing times.

We ran in rain and snow and sleet. We ran in 98° heat. We knocked out 22-mile, Saturday morning training runs. Teresa and I became best friends. As the news editor of a local daily newspaper, I began writing columns about her success. She wowed the international racing circuit with a 31:55 10K win at the Crescent City Classic in New Orleans, only seven seconds behind the American record in a 6.2 mile race, and began appearing in Runners' World magazine as a top contender in any race she ran. Norwegian record-breaking runners Grete Waitz and Ingrid Kristiansen had to pay attention to this unknown but determined runner from the Appalachian Mountains.

In July of 1987, the Los Angeles Times blasted a story on the eve of a major race about Teresa's unexpected arrival on the running circuit with a headline that read: OVERNIGHT SENSATION: Teresa Ornduff, 30, Hits Road-Running World by Storm.

Reporter Curt Holbreich wrote: "Just last year, Ornduff was little more than a 29-year-old competitive fitness freak from a small town in southwestern Virginia. Sunday, she'll enter the Carlsbad 5,000 as one of its leading entrants and with the year's second fastest time for an American woman for a 10-kilometer road race."

"Top runners were coming up to me asking, 'Where have you been? What have you been doing? Did you crawl out from the woodwork?' " Ornduff said earlier this week. "They were really curious about me. At first, they didn't take me seriously at all, but the way I've been running, they've got to take me seriously."

One year later, an Olympic year, Teresa Ornduff was fast enough to compete in both the women's Olympic Marathon Trials in Pittsburgh in May and the Olympic 10,000 Meter Trials in Indianapolis in July. I planned on being at both events to cheer her on. Would she make the US Olympic team and head to Seoul, South Korea? Only the top three finishers make the team; in distance running, it all comes down to how the body feels in that moment. Teresa, like every runner, was hoping her entire career would peak in either one of those races.

Unlike any other sport, most Olympic athletes have one and only one shot of a lifetime to earn that prize.

Ornduff was up against 206 other runners on May 2. The good news for the entire field was that 1984 Olympic gold medal champion Joan Samuelson wasn't in the pack. I had thrown my bike in the car and made the seven-hour trip to Pittsburgh to follow my training partner's pace and write about this moment for her friends back home.

Teresa's best marathon up to now was a 2:41:11 here in Pittsburgh. She knew she had to knock 10 minutes off that time to be competitive and possibly win a spot on the team. She knew the course well, and we had trained harder than ever to get her ready for this race.

In a marathon, you listen closely to your body because you know you'll experience a series of highs and lows during the 2 1/2 hours required to complete a 26-mile journey. Often times, the early pacemakers can't hold the lead because their bodies give out and they hit the wall.

Teresa knew that a 5 minute, 45 second pace might earn her that top three spot. That was her target, a 2:30 finishing time. So she didn't focus on the lead pack and its pace.

In the end, she drifted back just a bit, fell off her pace and wound up average 5:55 per mile to finish 12th in a time of 2 hours and 35 minutes in that field of 207 women runners. She had broken her personal best by six minutes. But she didn't make that Olympic team.

It was now time to allow her body to recover, ramp up her speed work on the track, and prepare for the 10,000-meter trials in Indianapolis in July. Teresa was making history with the other 10K competitors; this was the first ever women's Olympic 10K trials. And Teresa knew the competition would be even fiercer on the track than it was in Pittsburgh. She only ever raced the 10K distance on the road; the track would require speed and strategy, with arms flailing and every step requiring careful placement of her feet.

On that July evening, Teresa ran a sterling race in a time of 32 minutes and 55 seconds. But the top three finishers were a minute ahead of her. She came in 10th in the field, proud of her achievements at age 31. She clearly recognized that her running career likely peaked when it came to Olympic possibilities. The next round would be at age 35, an extreme long shot for someone like Teresa Ornduff who had emerged as an international star out of nowhere.

For me and my life of running, training and racing with a superstar runner was clearly an exclamation mark! Teresa knew all about our challenging journey with Beth; I shared every high and every low with her as we laid down mile after mile together. Teresa, a woman of strong faith, listened, then lifted me up during our toughest times.

In return, she shared with me that the courage we exhibited during these hard times - giving Beth every opportunity we could to maintain quality of life - gave her the push she needed to overcome any hurdles in her life and become the world class runner she was.

Road racing with Beth literally took our breath away!

# The Year Is 1991

Enduring a four-week illness that robs you of your ability to walk and eat, while under an assault of continuous grand mal seizures, is something few of us could survive.

It is February 1991, and our challenged daughter is almost 9 years old. She has spent her days in a trainable mentally handicapped classroom at Van Pelt Elementary School in Bristol, Virginia, and was training to run-walk the 50-meter dash at the Area X Special Olympics Games. Her mom and I had growing confidence that this would be a stellar moment - one of those highlights we could actually mark as a milestone in our daughter's lifetime.

Beth was prepping well for this event; it was still two months away and she was running more than walking when we set her little feet on the track and asked her to run to a greeter at the finish line! Heads up, Usain Bolt!

Her biggest confirmation to her dad that she was hitting the stretch run was when I picked her up at school one afternoon. Her classroom was in the rear of the school and actually had a back door that opened to a long sidewalk leading to a parking lot. I got out of my car in that parking lot and started up the sidewalk when I noticed the back door opening. Beth's one-on-one assistant, Peggy Dowdy, stepped outside with Beth and released her to me.

I stopped in my tracks, hoping that I might get my wish - my daughter hearing me call her name and then watching her head in my direction with joy spread across her face and determination unleashed in those little legs as she moved forward to greet me. And that's exactly what happened!

But this moment was more monumental than I had hoped. Beth took a few steady steps before hearing me shout her name. She then broke into a faster pace, a fast waddle, the fastest Beth has ever moved. A legitimate run? Oh, yes! I was witnessing an Olympic moment, a gold-medal-world-record-setting event! She made it all the way to the finish line, into my waiting arms. And I branded her my champion!

Unfortunately, this was the last time Beth would experience that kind of freedom on her feet. A week later, our daughter's life would change dramatically. She was sick with some kind of respiratory issue and would wind up in a local hospital with pneumonia. The physician examining her shocked us when he discharged her from his care, telling us a child like Beth, with her significant disabilities, is someone he simply didn't have time to care for.

And he was the only person in my life I ever wanted to physically hurt - but didn't.

We were stunned by this uncaring attitude, but had to focus on getting Beth well. So we turned immediately to Cindy's two oldest brothers, Marty, a pulmonologist, and Steve, an internist, who practiced together at a hospital in rural Southwest Virginia.

We needed genuine, compassionate medical care because we were headed down a near-death path that we never anticipated.

Beth grew weaker and began having clusters of seizures way beyond her normal pattern. Her body was stressed, and on day two of her hospitalization, we learned that our daughter had a case of thrush, a fungal infection that created white lesions inside her mouth and down her throat. Beth stopped eating immediately and didn't eat for the next eight months, even though the infection had been cured. Our fears centered on not only how to feed our daughter but how to effectively get her seizure medications to her. She could no longer take them orally.

The answer- a gastrostomy or feeding tube. The surgical procedure went well, but the unexpected bump was that Beth's front four teeth were knocked loose when the apparatus placed in her mouth during surgery was too large. She needed to lose those teeth anyway because she was 9 years old, but seeing her bloody mouth and those loosened teeth after this sudden feeding tube operation was another blow neither we, nor she, deserved.

Days at the hospital grew into weeks - four total - and Cindy and I began to fear the sudden loss of our dear daughter. The seizures occurred every time we moved Beth.

She was so vulnerable, we finally had to talk live-or-death issues with our medical team. Nine years of life with Beth were laced with so many medical hurdles and moments of simple glory. We wanted more of the latter, much more. But we expected no more.

We learned to fight heartache and find courage in almost any struggle life would hand us through this mysterious and undiagnosed child of ours. Beth taught us about a greater relevance in life than ourselves. She led Cindy and me to God, to an understanding that His plan is what we follow, and in doing so, we would be taught the true reason why we live. I definitely decided to ride her coattails to heaven.

And then Beth lived on.

She would never walk again on her own, and that feeding tube would be her lifeline in fighting seizures and maintaining nutrition to continue living. More struggles were ahead - and more miracles might happen. Beth wanted more from life. And she clearly became our blueprint for courage. We headed home. It was time to learn much more from her.

---

Nearly losing my broken baby girl so early in life was yet another harsh reminder that loss of family can and will happen. It certainly did in my life.

Growing up with five sisters and a brother in the modest Midwestern town of Hudson, Wisconsin, 20 miles from the Twin Cities along the St. Croix River, I was a happy-go-lucky kid, skinny enough to be nicknamed "Spinny" and homely, highlighted by a huge gap - like footballer Michael Strahan's - between my front two teeth.

Mom and dad wanted a large family - and they wanted it fast! That happened. Mary was born in 1954, Luke in '55, twins Anne and Sarah in '56 and I arrived 11 months later on May 1 in 1957. Helen was born two years later followed by the only unexpected child, Gemma, five years later.

We were tight-knit siblings who played cops-and-robbers and kick-the-can and red-rover in a spacious yard just outside the town limits. We walked to the library every Saturday morning to compete in the monthly book-reading competition. Reading 15 short books a week wasn't difficult for any of us! We played baseball in the shadow of two huge pine trees and climbed those 60-foot trees when we felt bold and adventuresome. We walked to school, both ways, a mile each way, and it wasn't uphill.

We also raised Bantam chickens, dozens of them, and generation upon generation. Our parents let us pick our favorites and call them our own. We fed them in their chicken coops and rounded them up at night from the lilac bushes in our back yard. We treated them like pets, tying strings to their legs to "take them for walks" and sliding down Coon's Hill on cardboard boxes with them in our laps. At the end of the ride, we'd get up, clean off our laps from the mess they made, and head back up the hill for more fun.

We gathered up the eggs they laid to feed our family of nine - and accepted the reality that these chickens would also feed our family, even the ones we "owned" as our favorites. Mine was a solid black rooster named "Nippy."

Mom and dad warned us when it was time to take one down for dinner. Looking back now, the chicken slaughter was somewhat shocking and graphic! My parents would capture their next victim from the coop, carry it behind the garage and wring its neck. We kids never witnessed the "assassination of our pets" but we knew it wasn't pretty because that headless chicken would come flying from around the garage into the yard, blood flying everywhere, until it flapped a final few times and gave up the ghost. Moments later, the dead fowl would be dropped into a pot of boiling water. We would be encouraged to help pluck the wet feathers from that rubbery bird and then get it cooked as the main entree for dinner that night!

Dad, who grew up on a farm in South Dakota, was a doctor. Mom, who grew up on a farm in North Dakota, was a nurse. And we were a playful, loving family that sorrow simply couldn't touch.

But it did in 1966, by way of a drunk driver who snatched the life from my brother, Luke, outside the playground of St. Patrick's School. The way I remember the day, it was a gray Friday, and Luke, 11 years young at the time, was asked by one of the nuns at school to run an errand to the downtown pharmacy after school on his bike.

The street beside St. Pat's was all uphill, and on this particular day, Oct. 18, cars were lining the right side of the street, blocking most of the view of the school playground and entrance. Mrs. Knox - the name I remember as a nine-year-old - drove up the street in an inebriated state. Mom and Dad would later learn that she was moving along about 35 miles per hour - or 20 miles an hour over the speed limit. There was no opportunity for her to stop if she saw a youngster from the school suddenly appear on a bike in her path. And that's exactly what happened.

A most profound irony occurred next, but it was something I wouldn't find out until years later when I explored the details of this tragedy through my mother's vivid memories. Dad, a pediatrician, was on call at the hospital when Luke's bike slammed into the Knox car, throwing him over his handlebars and across the top of the vehicle. He landed hard on his head on the asphalted street on the other side of the car. Witnesses said he lay motionless.

The call went out to the small Hudson hospital, and Dad rushed to the scene on St. Croix Street to find a stunned crowd gathered near Luke. Little did my father know that he'd find his own son fighting for his very life.

I never found out how Dad handled this shocking discovery. I do recall that he was stoic for his five daughters and me. I know that we saw little of him and Mom for the next 48 hours. They were standing at Luke's bedside in an ICU unit in some large hospital in St. Paul, Minnesota, praying for a miracle they knew wouldn't happen. My older brother, gentle and kind in his youthful state, was in a coma from which he would not recover.

On October 20th, 1966, Luke was called to heaven. That's what Dad told us, in those exact words. Our brother - my best friend who'd taught me how to make rabbit traps and build campfires in the fields next to our big country home - was gone to a secure place where love and comfort were constant. Heaven, Dad told us, was exactly where Luke belonged. I agree - but that doesn't mean I didn't miss his strong mentoring and close companionship.

That was personal tragedy number one. At age nine, I didn't really recognize it as such. I was a bit confused about the attention our family received from the community in the small town where we lived. I wasn't even sure that this kind of accident didn't happen to every Midwestern family.

The dark cloud was hovering over me, but I was too young to look skyward and fear its menacing presence.

Phil with sisters, Helen, Gemma, Sarah, Anne and mother Rose gather in Orlando just after Phil's diagnosis.

### The Year is 1992

When Jeffrey Prince was eight years old, or maybe nine, he sat in the back seat of his mom's car and heard the two most important women in his life play the "what if" game by expressing their greatest fears as mothers.

Sister Cindy spoke her mind first. She was 16 at the time.

"If I become a mom, my biggest fear is to have a child who's handicapped. I just don't think I could handle that."

To which her mother, Phyllis, who had an established family of five sons and one daughter, responded: "That I could handle. What I couldn't deal with is a child who is queer."

Today, at 45, Jeffrey Prince knows why that conversation stuck with him - perhaps more than any other he's overheard in life.

---

"So guess what Jeff told me?" my wife of 13 years asked me as she entered our home through the back door. It was obvious by the tone in her voice that whatever her 27-year-old brother had shared with her had been a heavyweight topic. And she definitely wasn't expecting anything more from me than a "what?"

Cindy had been gone for two solid hours. Jeff, the youngest of her five brothers, had warned her that he wanted to talk about something "pretty heavy" that evening. It was obvious by the look on her face when she came in from the dark of night that what they'd discussed was having a profound affect on her.

"He's gay, isn't he?" I said with a straight face and a matter-of-fact tone to my voice.

Cindy's jaw dropped and she stopped in her tracks. "How did you know? You didn't tell me you knew that."

I didn't know. And I hadn't speculated before now. It's what came to my head and out of my mouth at that particular moment, almost before I even realized the magnitude of my statement. It was one of those moments that just happens, when you hit the jackpot answer on one of the most significant questions you've ever been asked and never expected that your answer would be the right one. What if my answer had been wrong? That would have stung Cindy. Instead, I was dead on.

I'd delivered a larger-than-life answer to a question that would change my wife's perspective on difference and diversity forever, planting her firmly on the side of support no matter what, love no matter what, devotion no matter what. It changed her comfortable, conservative political views and her fundamentalist religious views on a dime. Her perspectives were instantly altered. Her brother was gay.

She loved Jeff and would grow to understand his lifestyle and believe the story he told about what brought him to that place in life at age 27.

That would take some educating on our part. The white elephant in the room was the ominous question: Has he told his mom and dad? I think we would have known.

But before we got to that question, I asked my wife another one. "Do you mind if I call Jeff and tell him I love him?"

And so I did. Here's a kid - or rather a young man - whose confusion level the past 15 years had to have been off the charts. Regardless of how I felt about the gay population in 1992 - and, in fact, I didn't really give it a whole lot of serious thought because I was too consumed with caring for that "handicapped child" my wife had feared having - I needed to let my brother-in-law know how I truly felt about him.

This was the kid who, when young, would hang around his only sister and her date - that would be me - incessantly. I couldn't shake the kid. This threesome was popular at the movies, the local burger joints, and the ballgames. He was attached to Cindy's hip, needing to be part of her life, needing her guidance as a mother figure after her mother suffered a near-fatal brain hemorrhage at age 42.

It was no wonder that when Jeff broke through the fear of "coming out" as a gay man, he would break the news first and foremost to his reliably strong and supportive sister.

It was sister before Mom and Dad, not because he didn't love and respect his parents. He adored them. He viewed them as community pillars.

It's just that he was absolutely certain of his sister's reaction. But his parents? His mind raced back to that day in the back seat of the car, when his mother uttered those words: "What I couldn't handle is a child who is queer."

His father was a man who had stumbled with a three-year bout with an alcohol addiction when his six children were at very formative ages. And he had pushed through it - with determination and tough love from his wife - to establish a 50-plus year career as a dentist in the coal-mining town of Wise, Virginia. In the long run, he would become one of the most admired figures in the community. He was my new father when Cindy and I started dating at age 16. Today he is my 40-year father.

Jeff looked at his mother as a brave woman who had stared down death on more than one occasion to be a strong, guiding voice to every one of her children as they headed to Blacksburg to attend Virginia Tech. Cancer scares and the daily aches and pains from the hemorrhage in the prime of her life had her fighting for some semblance of normalcy for almost half a century - from age 42 to age 80 plus.

---

Jeff pondered those words he'd heard from the backseat of mom's car. His sister feared most having a child with disabilities. And now she has a child who isn't just a bit disabled; her infant daughter Elizabeth suffered from a complex neuromuscular disorder that robbed her of her ability to talk and walk at a young age. Her life is complicated with a lifetime of severe grand mal seizures, scoliosis, osteoporosis, poor circulation of the extremities, breathing dysfunctions, hand wringing, a short life expectancy, a rare bone disorder affecting both feet, and on and on it went.

The adjustment was transforming for Jeff's sister. In fact, it led her to the professional career of education - special education, to be exact. The education of preschool aged children with disabilities and behavioral problems.

Would his mother handle her "ultimate in irony" statement as gracefully as her daughter handled her true-to-life experience of raising a child with multiple disabilities?

Would she shun the child who winds up proclaiming he's homosexual at a time when "coming out" was a risky public proclamation from many angles? Jeff held down a full-time job at a four-year university. He lived in a small southern town in the heart of the Bible belt. Acceptance would come few and far between. Judge and jury would be out in full force to condemn him. He knew all that, but he'd become his own person.

Meanwhile, Jeff relied on sister Cindy to be the proper gauge for when the time was right, if there was a right time, to break the news to his parents. Months went by without a truthful confession.

And then one morning he picked up the local newspaper and came across a poem called "The Man in the Glass." It spoke to him that the time was right - that "the world made him king for a day." He vowed to take full advantage of how Peter Dale Winbrow, Sr. spoke to him that day in the local daily paper. The time was right to make a memorable trip from Bristol over to Wise County that evening to break some important news to his parents.

## The Man In The Glass
### Peter "Dale" Winbrow Sr.

When you get what you want in your struggle for self
And the world makes you king for a day,
Just go to the mirror and look at yourself
And see what that man has to say.

For it isn't your father or mother or wife
Whose judgment upon you must pass?
The fellow whose verdict counts most in you life
Is the one staring back from the glass.

You may be like Jack Horner and chisel a plum
And think you're a wonderful guy.
But the man in the glass says you're only a bum
If you can't look him straight in the eye.

He's the fellow to please-never mind all the rest,
For he's with you clear to the end.
And you've passed your most dangerous, difficult test
If the man in the glass is your friend.

You may fool the whole world down the pathway of years
And get pats on the back as you pass.
But your final reward will be heartache and tears
If you've cheated the man in the glass.

Jeff wasn't going to cheat himself of this opportunity. He was ready for any outcome - good or bad. He was ready for an embrace or a stiff-arm. He would embrace words of endearment and cringe at words of hatred and misunderstanding. But he had prepared himself to take any and all of it.

He certainly knew the reaction from his mom and dad wasn't going to be indifference. He was ready for flight if they simply didn't accept his lot in life. He was hoping for acceptance - or at least a grain of understanding, with the opportunity for some educating so that a mere 27 years of life wouldn't be the end of a relationship with powerfully strong and influential parents.

His parents had shown they had the ability to stare down adversity and put love first. In the case of daughter Cindy, they'd pushed tough love after our baby Beth was born, encouraging her to get out of the house and explore a career opportunity that would help her balance life with - or without - Beth. With her husband's alcohol problem, Phyllis had looked the other way on more occasions than she could possibly recall. She loved him despite repeated failures on his part.

With their baby boy, they'd been down a tough path as well. Jeffrey was born with a pretty severe facial birth defect - a cleft lip that required numerous operations in a big city far from the coalfields of Wise County.

Their journey was scary at times. It required bravery from Phyllis and John, and the hope that their little boy's face could be restored to something close to normal so that he could breath, eat, chew, swallow and talk without too much interference. And if all that happened, he wouldn't be ridiculed either.

---

Jeff arrived at his parents' home in Wise at dinnertime. The adrenaline was flowing. John and Phyllis were happy their son was paying them a visit on a weeknight. Dinner was served. And then Jeff delivered the shocking news.

"I'm gay. I've always been gay; I love you and want to be part of this family, but you need to be okay with this or I won't be coming around much anymore."

It was the cold hard truth.

Jeff had years to process who he was and it wasn't fair to expect his parents to immediately accept the news. Not surprisingly, their reaction wasn't accepting. They said they still loved Jeff but they needed time to sort things out.

Jeff left Wise that evening with a heavy and uncertain heart. Things went from bad to worse. His mother and dad were still subsidizing him financially, and he learned that his father wanted to put an end to that financial assistance; essentially, they were considering writing him off. Communication ended for at least a couple weeks, and Cindy became the intermediary between Jeff and his parents.

"I remember being disappointed and hurt, but I was resolved that I had done the right thing and that I would be okay either way," Jeff shared. His father, a respected dentist in this small town, was concerned that his practice might be negatively impacted if people found out that his youngest son was gay.

Ultimately, love endured. With the help of a couple of his sons, Jeff's father began to see a more accepting perspective toward his son's sexual orientation. He called Jeff and wanted him to pay another visit to Wise. Jeff sensed there might be a turnaround in his parents' understanding of who he really was.

"During that visit, he became my dad again," Jeff said.

Phyllis wasn't there yet - until she decided to take the family to see the movie Philadelphia, a 1993 film starring Denzel Washington and Tom Hanks. The movie plot was about a gay man with AIDS who was fired by a conservative law firm because of his condition. In turn, he hired a homophobic small-time lawyer as the only willing advocate for a wrongful dismissal suit.

After watching the movie, Phyllis gathered her family together and shared the following turnaround message with them: "The Tom Hanks family in that film, that's the kind of family we are and that's the kind of family we need to be for Jeff." She issued a matriarchal decree that it was okay by her that Jeff was gay and everyone else needed to get with the program! From that day forward, she became her son's biggest defender and champion.

"What I've often told Mom and Dad is that they always emphasized unconditional love when we were growing up and, in my case, when put to the test, they came through with flying colors," Jeff said. "I have so many friends who either have no relationship with their families of origin or who remain closeted and choose to edit their lives; I think either scenario is incredibly damaging to a person's soul and sense of self.

"Looking at it today, coming out of the closet doesn't seem like such a big deal, but in the early '90s when I told Mom and Dad, we were still in the pre-Ellen DeGeneres and 'Will and Grace' era, the AIDS crisis was raging and homophobia was really at a fevered pitch. I don't think I've done many brave or bold things in my life, but I'll always consider the decision to live openly during such a time to be a significant act of courage and, in some small way, a real contribution to making our country a better place."

Jeff's ultimate take on how to live is this: he believes it is important to lead a principled life, treat others as he wishes to be treated, contribute what he can to his community, and take good care of those around him.

That perspective was truly honored years later when Jeff was awarded a statewide human rights award in North Carolina for giving all that he could in the city of Greensboro in pushing successful fundraising to support victims struggling with AIDS.

By "coming out" to his sister, Cindy, at age 27, Jeff Prince, with partner Michael Jolly, changed the perspective about diversity within the Prince family.

My marathon years were over in the early '90s, but I had shifted gears with the encouragement of a new training partner, my dear brother-in-law and extraordinary competitor, Phillip Prince. He was five years younger than me, and he and I had raced against each other in the shorter distance races in the 1980s. He wasn't a marathoner but could put those feet down fast in 5K and 10K races. He also began cycling as the world of biathlons and triathlons began heating up.

I had my running down pat; my endurance was well established. I had run six marathons, each one faster than the previous, and had put in more than 25,000 miles on my feet. I had run dozens and dozens of 5K, 10K, 15 K, 10 mile, and half marathon races. Now I had to learn how to draft in a peloton,

push myself up long, steep mountain grades on a cycle, and
grow fearless as I plunged down the other side of those steep
mountain roads at speeds of up to 50 mph. This brother-in-law
was the one who would train me to accomplish these feats.

I was always a few strides faster than Phillip on my legs,
and he was quicker on the bike than I was. The one who
reached the finish line first between the two of us was
determined by the length of the run versus the length of the
cycling event at each race. There were times when a biathlon
would begin with a run and I would establish a 15 or 20 second
lead on Phillip. We would then transition onto our cycles and
within a mile or two, my brother-in-law would ease by me and
take the lead, always encouraging me to push as hard as I could
as he passed me. I would try to keep him within sight, with the
hope that I could catch him on that second run. Strategy was a
big key to our success; Phillip tackled uphills both on foot and
on cycle quicker than I did. I was faster on the downhills than
he was.

Sometimes I would hit the line first, and sometimes he
would hold me off and cross that finish line ahead of me. But
we were always just seconds apart. And regardless of the
outcome, we shared the exhilaration of racing against one
another. Our embraces to each other were sincere. And yes,
every race literally took our breath away!

Our greatest biathlon experience occurred at Lake
Lanier north of Atlanta in the Coors Light Biathlon Series
during the summer of 1992. We had trained hard for this elite
race, knowing that the best biathletes in the world, including
the number one competitor, Ken Souza, from Canada would be
toeing the starting line with us.

It was a warm Saturday morning, and thousands of racers were ready to put it all out on the line. Phillip and I were among them. Our cycles were primed, our legs were rested, and our minds were prepped for something great.

The opening 5K was tougher than I expected; it was hilly and worked on my mind. Phillip worked it well, and he and I pulled into the transition area side-by-side. I jumped on my Mongoose, my brother-in-law in my peripheral vision. We heard that the 30K bike ride wasn't going to be an easy venture. It was a killer for me; I had an unexpected drop in my energy level, but I kept pushing hard to try to keep up with my brother-in-law.

A moment that took my breath away was when Liz Browning, the top female biathlete in the world, cycled by me halfway through the race. I looked to my left as I felt someone rolling by me with ease. I didn't expect it to be Browning and I didn't expect her to blow by me with such a smooth approach.

She crushed my confidence. Should I expect to keep up with the fastest, most accomplished female biathlete in the world? Clearly not. But the simplicity in which she passed me left me with some doubt about conquering the second half of this important race.

Phillip was obviously feeling strong, having disappeared out ahead of me. I needed to find the drive and desire to finish this race, as I had done many times over in previous races.

I dug down deep and pushed through the rest of a roller coaster cycling segment, tossed my bike beside, jumped back into my racing flats, and tackled that tough 5K course on foot to finish 24th. I was proud of that finish, but was even prouder that Phillip was waiting at the finish line for me, cheering me on. He had finished 20th against a monster field. I was more than proud of his accomplishment!

We would continue to race against each other, the outcomes always uncertain but exciting. The exceptional part of this relationship was that it wasn't about who finished number one; it was all about turning that brother-in-law status into a brotherly love that would deepen over the years and require a "never give up" status between the two of us for a couple of important reasons.

In 2010, Phillip lost his closest cycling training partner, Bill Collie, to a sudden heart attack while the two were on a training ride on a back road in Wise County. Bill had a history of heart issues but raced at a very high level. He was doing what he loved best when his heart gave out.

A year later, my terminal illness diagnosis was another crushing blow to Phillip Prince. He did not want to lose another close friend, someone he spent hours on the road burning endorphins together and soaking up memories with a training partner. He has driven me to fight all out. He insists that I never give up.

## The Year Is 1993

Life seemed to move along in a blur the first three years after Luke's death. That tragedy hit us hardest at Christmas when he wasn't there to sing carols with us by candlelight around the tree. That memory was most vivid to me.

Meanwhile, Leo and Rose Timp - dad and mom - were developing a definitive game plan to move the family somewhere down South, a move that would profoundly affect the rest of my life.

We couldn't have been adequately forewarned of the culture shock we would experience with this move. Our red and white Volkswagen bus was packed to the nines, and we pulled a camper trailer that gave us a place to bed down during our three-day journey to the central Appalachian Mountain region.

Days one and two were mostly uneventful, although we did experience a significant scare on the buzzing freeway through Chicago when our camper trailer jumped off the hitch and weaved dangerously close to passing 18-wheelers somewhere on I-94 near Lake Michigan. Dad was mostly calm as he pulled the car and trailer off the highway to safety. As an adult today with a wife and three children, I don't know that I'd have handled that near disaster as reassuring as my father did. I don't remember any panic in his voice. He just got us to safety with very little fanfare.

Things got scary for us in a much different way as we hit the bluish-green mountains of eastern Kentucky. The fear was where Dad had taken us!

Four-lane roads became two-lane roller coaster climbs and downhill plunges into steep curves. But any progress was blunted by a line of chugging coal trucks straining to make it to the top of the next of many peaks.

We were making our way - slow and measured - through the Appalachian Mountains for the first time ever, and it was an eerie experience. Who lived in these soot-covered hollers? As kids, we stared in disbelief at toilet paper, trash and discarded clothing hanging off the low-hanging branches along the creek beds we motored by.

Tears stung our eyes. We asked Dad where we were headed. Surely we'd pass through this dark, angry piece of land - our Jurassic Park adventure - and arrive at a bright, scenic pastoral place when we arrived in Virginia. Not so. Wise County in 1969 was experiencing another black gold boon, metallurgical coal mined by the thousands of tons daily to be shipped overseas to places like China and India where steel was in huge demand.

We kids never figured out how Dad found this place. It was much later that we would learn that Dad's missionary mentality led his desire to practice pediatric medicine in poverty stricken Appalachia. This was a much different corner of the world, a place that would create culture shock for a Midwestern family, but it was a place that I eventually recognized as "God's Country."

I was 12 years old and in seventh grade when we moved to Wise, Virginia, and I will never forget the three 18-year-olds in my homeroom class who wore leather and chains every day to school. At the end of the day, they would roll out the window of our basement level classroom and fake a brutal fistfight on the playground, drawing big crowds of legitimate seventh graders in awe of their size, strength and brutality.

We missed Luke, but most of us in this family of eight adapted well to a whole new world. Change is part of living, and on April 29, 1972, life threw our family another wicked curveball.

It was a Saturday evening, and mom, dad and my five sisters - Mary, twin sisters Anne and Sarah, Helen and Gemma - headed to J.J. Kelly High School for a ballet performance. I chose to stay home to listen to a radio play-by-play of an Atlanta Braves baseball game. I was hot on America's Pastime and was playing the game myself as a freshman on the Kelly baseball team.

Two hours later, life changed dramatically for our family. My sisters burst through the front door of the house, wailing with the horrifying news that dad was dead. My father, who was on call that evening, left the ballet performance early after receiving a page that a sick child needed his attention. After attending to this patient, dad went into his office to document information about the child, and then began having chest pain. He contacted his closest physician friend, Dr. Sid Sewell, about his concerns with his health. Sid rushed to the hospital, only to find Leo Timp experiencing a massive heart attack. Resuscitation efforts were put into full effect, but my dad didn't make it.

At age 46, he was gone from our lives, and my mother, a woman of unmatched determination, was on her own in raising her remaining six children. Dad, a native of De Smet, South Dakota, was laid to rest in a valley rimmed by breathtaking walls of mountain beauty outside Big Stone Gap, Virginia. These mountains of strength mirrored my dad's spiritual foundational strength. It was most definitively a virtue he passed on to me, and one I have passed onto my children.

Musical theater was always an attraction for me because I loved singing, even as a youngster in a church choir anywhere we lived. We weren't a musical family, per se, like the Von Trapps. But my mother always sang with passion at church, and my sisters and I would join in by belting it out as youngsters every chance we had. I remember performing the song "Do You Hear What I Hear" with my sisters at St. Anthony's Catholic Church in Norton, Virginia, on Christmas Eve at Mass.

In high school, I was one of a few males who sang in the high school choir and just missed making the state choir as a senior. I went on to sing in the glee club in college at Washington and Lee University. But singing wasn't the only "on stage" presence I enjoyed. I loved acting even more, and we were led in high school by Jim Dotson, a flamboyant theater director who would later die of AIDS after moving to Charlottesville, Virginia.

We were big on the Broadway musical Pippin, copying their white face and leotard look on a high school stage in the early 1970s! As a four-sport athlete, I can't believe I wasn't ostracized by my teammates. After two hours of round ball competition on the hardwood court during the winter or taking batting practice until the palms of my hands were bleeding on the baseball diamond in the spring, I would join up with a different set of classmates on stage to rehearse song and dance numbers to prepare for the one act state competition in theater.

Cindy and I were often on stage together as lead actress and actor in our high school performances. We often walked away at play festivals with the top award and top individual performances. "Coach" Dotson took it a step further by training us in what at that time was called the forensics competition, which included boys and girls poetry, prose, a spelling competition and extemporaneous speaking.

Cindy performed brilliantly and finished second in the state in girls prose with a heart-thumping performance from Alfred Hitchcock's thriller called "Sorry, Wrong Number." I was in Charlottesville at the state competition with her and several other classmates, trying my best to defeat a young African American kid from a nearby high school who had beaten me in both the district and regional competitions in boy's poetry. His voice was smooth and silky, and he deserved those first-place finishes. At state, however, the tables surprisingly turned, and I upset him to grab first place with my performance of Vachel Lindsay's Negro spiritual titled, "How Sampson Bore Away the Gates of Gaza."

We were drawing rave reviews on stage and getting standing ovations, and I was having as much fun or more than I did on the playing fields at JJ Kelly - and I was extraordinarily passionate on the track, the tennis court, the baseball diamond and in the gym shooting hoops.

In my adult life, opportunities to sing at weddings were more than a highlight. Being chosen to play gospel writer Luke in an Easter cantata called "Once Upon A Tree" written by Raleigh music minister Pepper Choplin brought me a whole lot closer to the reality of the suffering, sacrificial death and glorious resurrection of Jesus Christ. With an orchestra and a 150-member choir behind me, I "lived and breathed" this story on stage at the brand-new Meymandi Concert Hall in Raleigh. Our performance drew a standing ovation. My role as a writer of biblical history seemed surreal. At one point, I "broke character" and wept on stage as I felt the reality of the song

"Crucify," feeling like I would have given in to the crowd's unrelenting pursuit of this innocent man named Jesus. Would I have berated him, scorned him as he stumbled and fell, that huge cross crushing him on that road to Calvary?

I played another biblical role on stage a few years earlier and created quite a memory for my family.

It happened at a small community theater in Bristol, Tennessee, in 1993 during a dress rehearsal performance of Andrew Lloyd Webber's "Joseph and the Amazing Technicolor Dreamcoat."

I was excited to have a role in this musical. It was one of my favorite Broadway shows, and, at the age of 35, I knew I wasn't going to be one of the 12 sons of Jacob. But maybe I could grab the role of Captain Potiphar, who would rage on Joseph, accusing him of coming after Mrs. Potiphar and jailing him for actions he never committed.

That's the role I landed, the character of a man I could never be but one I would enjoy on stage. Captain Potiphar had a soft-shoe shuffle and solo to perform just before intermission. I would enter stage right in an Egyptian pose, left hand flattened out in front of me, right hand flattened out behind me. Marching on stage behind me was Mrs. Potiphar in the same pose. We would move to center stage and begin our dance. I would belt out the lyrics and the entire cast, on stage behind us, would play out the words I sang.

I had the chance to draw a big round of applause and get the crowd excited for a powerful second half performance.

Our kids were young at that time, Joseph the youngest at age 4, and all three were in attendance - along with another 150 people - at our Thursday night dress rehearsal. Opening night was around the corner, and I had been practicing song and dance at home to the extent that the kids knew my lines by heart. They knew the dance, too.

The show opened on that Thursday night with tremendous energy. Our Joseph had a sterling tenor voice and his brothers had their stuff together, singing and dancing to a crowd of friends and family who had received special invitations to this event.

And then it was time for Potiphar to perform. I took a deep breath, jumped into my Egyptian pose and off I went with Mrs. Potiphar to kill our number! Kill it I did, but in a much different way!

My opening line was easy, it made sense, and it was my introduction of who I was: "Potiphar had very few cares; he was one of Egypt's millionaires, having made a fortune buying shares in pyramids."

But I didn't sing that line. Instead, I opened with the second verse, shocking my fellow actors and actresses and confusing them in what to do on stage behind me.

"Potiphar was cool and so fine, but his wife would never toe the line. It's all there in Chapter 39 of Genesis."

And then it hit me; I was wrong with my words. I flashed my eyes left and right, and my brain told my body to stop dancing. How would I get this right when it was all wrong? I had NOT rehearsed this moment.

Impromptu! Do something quick and make it right, Captain Potiphar! Make the audience laugh; keep them from feeling your pain!

So I took a quick glance behind me and then motioned to our orchestra in the pit. My words were simple and direct: "Well, let's take it from the top, Mr. Director!"

And so we did.

When we arrived at intermission, I made a huge apology to the cast back stage. They had no regrets for my bumbling, stumbling performance. But there was someone in the audience who did.

Four-year-old son Joseph knew something had gone awry. He had witnessed me roll through this number at home far too many times. And so he took "center stage" on his mother's lap and hollered out to everyone around him: "My daddy messed up the whole play, didn't he, mommy?"

The crowd exploded in laughter; I had not drawn rave reviews from my baby boy. But I did learn a big lesson in better preparation for opening night! From that point on with each performance, I wrote my opening line on my left wrist, which was right in front of my eyes as I did my Egyptian strut on stage.

I was flawless from that point on!

---

I've talked about miracles happening in our lives through Beth. As parent advocates, we always kept our eyes and ears open to possibilities.

Next up? March 18, 1993. This one - at age 11 - was bigger than most. And I didn't dare walk away from that "moment" because it was miraculous and monumental in every sense of the word. It spread like a virus from classroom to classroom at that elementary school on that transformational spring morning.

Mickey Vanderwerker, a speech communications specialist from Virginia Tech's Training and Technical Assistance Center, came to Bristol, Virginia, to pay a visit to Van Pelt Elementary School and see what our daughter Beth had to offer. She'd heard that our pre-teen couldn't talk and had a lot of trouble separating her hands to functionally use them.

We still had no answer as to why our daughter needed to keep her hands tightly clasped and to herself. Oh, those hands were plenty busy; they were almost always in constant motion. It was just that she rarely separated them to use them to her benefit.

There were no medical answers at this point in her life. The debilitating combination of hands, seizures, evolving scoliosis, poor circulation in her feet, breathing dysfunction, non-verbal, non-ambulatory - it all just didn't have a name. And when you can't name this kind of frustration, it can be paralyzing.

And now someone who called herself a communications expert wanted to come into our daughter's life, believing she could make a difference by showing Beth a communication method called facilitated communication. FC was an avenue of communication useful for people who not only couldn't speak but also had trouble controlling their arm or hand motions to be able to functionally use them. Some of the most appropriate candidates were people with cerebral palsy who struggled with getting their body to cooperate with what their mind was telling them to do.

The idea behind FC is this: create an opportunity for an individual who struggles with hand and arm control to point on a communication board. It's touted as an all or nothing process. To allow Beth to do this, the facilitator had to sit next to our motorically challenged daughter and help her establish a "place in space" with one hand poised over a communication board in front of her. Mickey would place her hand firmly in the palm of

Beth's hand and ask her a question. If Beth was able to move her hand to the board, Mickey - with the slightest movement forward - would release all pressure from Beth's hand and allow her freedom of movement to point to her answer on the communications board.

It's a process that must be guarded against facilitator influence. Beth had to show definitive motion forward to make this legitimate.

Mickey shared with us that she had far too much experience - and success - with this process not to give Beth a shot at it. Beth's combination of no expressive language and hand wringing might be more than Mickey could tackle. But what could it hurt? We were at point zero in the area of effective communication with Beth Timp. The seemingly simple process of just separating Beth's hands was, to us, as complex as solving a Rubik's cube.

Mickey's most important question to me was which hand did Beth favor if she ever separated her hands. The left hand, I told her.

Then she got right to it, sitting down with Beth and explaining to her that trust and confidence was important in why she was going to separate Beth's hands, place a small pointer on her left index finger and then place her hand in Beth's left hand to give her a sense of confidence and actual ability to move her hand forward and point to one of four color blocks in front of her.

Mickey emphasized to Beth that when Beth chose to move her hand forward, Mickey would release all pressure off her hand and let her go where she wanted to go.

"Where's the red block," Mickey asked Beth. Our daughter's hand shot forward and she slammed her pointer finger on the red block. "How about the blue one." Yes! And the green and yellow blocks? Beth nailed it!

I took a deep breath, and some doubt entered my mind. A child with an IQ of 25 - would she even push her hand forward in back to back to back to back efforts with an IQ that low? And was it just a coincidence that she hit each color correctly?

Mickey looked over her shoulder at me to let me know Beth's movement was very definitive toward the board.

"I'd like to challenge her a little more with a letter board, and here's what I have in mind," Mickey said. She reached down in her bag and pulled out an A-thru-Z letter board with a "yes" and a "no" on opposite sides. Mickey lauded Beth for her success on the color chart and re-emphasized her confidence in what Beth might be able to accomplish going forward with this letter chart.

Then she dropped the bombshell on me, asking Beth if she knew how to spell her name. Without hesitation, Beth's finger shot forward to the letter B. She followed it up quickly with a poke at the letter E, then T, then H. But she didn't stop there.

She pointed to an I. Mickey told me later she thought Beth was going to point to an E next, because we still called Beth Bethie. But she didn't point to an E. She pointed instead to an A and then an M.

And she closed out her miracle statement with an S, followed by M-A-R-T!

I nearly melted in the floor, not really believing what I just witnessed and not wanting to give Beth the true credit for what she had just told me. Who is this Ouija queen, coming into our lives unannounced to knock the props out from under us after we had spent the first 11 years of life coping with the child we were told we had?

I said, "Mickey, did that really happen, and I mean happen on its own?"

"Sit down here, Doubting Thomas, and give Beth the chance to show you what she knows."

I took my seat next to my daughter, who was still looking at the letter board in front of her. She appeared to be mesmerized by its power and potential in her life.

"Ask her a question," Mickey said.

"Who is the president of the United States," I asked Beth. I felt her hand begin to separate from mine and I dropped mine from hers. C-L-I-N-T-O-N was her answer. It was 1993 and Bill Clinton was in his first of eight years of presidency. "What is his wife's name?"
H-I-L-A-R-Y. I forgave her for leaving that second L out of Hillary Clinton's name.

"Is there anything you'd like to say to your sister, Katie," I questioned her next. Katie is three years younger than Beth, and was eight years old at the time. Katie had an unusually close and protective attachment to her older sister.

Beth's message made my heart explode! F-I-N-A-L-L-Y K-A-T-I-E R-E-A-L-L-Y H-A-S A S-I-S-T-E-R!

Beth's one-on-one assistant, Peggy Dowdy, was so overwhelmed with emotion, she had to leave the room. I asked Beth if there was anything she wanted to share with Peggy, her special mentor. Her answer was beyond belief.

D-O-N-T W-O-R-R-Y A-B-O-U-T P-A-S-T, Beth prophesied. F-U-T-U-R-E!

Word spread throughout Van Pelt like a California wildfire. Teachers jumped from their classrooms to share their shock and awe with each other in the teachers' lounge. Emotions were high as Van Pelt's teachers fell into each others arms sobbing with joy at what just happened in Nancy Brown's classroom.

---

Did we ever move ahead! Beth gave us a strong directive, and we took it to heart to make her life incredibly rich and rewarding. The challenges with her physical disabilities, including her neurological episodes that were completely unpredictable, were as great as they ever were as she headed into her teenage years.

But there was one aspect of her life - a gate of cognition opening up to us - that we took full advantage of to improve her quality of life. The world of educational inclusion, the opportunity for Beth to be part of a regular classroom and share her unique and selective characteristics with her fellow students, was now a grand opportunity for her.

Beth left her trainable mentally handicapped classroom and became part of a fifth grade class at Van Pelt Elementary. The remaining two months of the year were supreme for her, and she confirmed time and time again that the March 18 miracle wasn't just a one-hit wonder!

She arrived at school one morning in a sour mood, and her teaching assistant asked her what was bothering her. She spelled out M-O-M M-A-D M-O-N-E-Y! Later that afternoon, teacher Nancy Brown, who always gave us a daily update on what Beth's day was like, called Cindy. The conversation went like this: "I don't mean to get into your's and Phil's personal situations, but Beth was upset about something this morning I need to run it by you to find out if it was legit," Nancy said chuckling. "She spelled out "Mom mad money. What was that about?"

Cindy broke into laughter. There was no hesitation in her recollection of our loud argument the night before about finances. We didn't know it triggered irritation in our daughter, who was in the next room listening to our overwhelming discussion about what to do with our financial picture.

"I guess Beth's message to us was 'you don't have to raise your voices when you disagree about something,'" Cindy shared with Nancy.

We witnessed another powerful affirmation of the value of facilitated communication on the Monday following Mother's Day. In simple general conversation, Beth was asked what her mother received as a Mother's Day gift. She spelled out W-H-I-T-E F-L-O-W-E-R. Later that day, Cindy received her afternoon phone call from Ms. Brown, who told her it was nice that Beth recalled that she had received a white flower for Mother's Day. Cindy scratched her head, then shared with Nancy that she had received a nice electric mixer from the kids and that Beth had used a switch to help power the mixer and make a cake for her. "White flower" perhaps was intended to be "white flour," the cake mix.

Later that evening, I arrived home from work and Cindy shared the "white flower" story with me. I paused briefly, and then it hit me. "Cindy, do you remember what Reverend Jones asked all mothers to do as they left church yesterday morning on Mother's Day? Take a white carnation from the vase as you left church!

"That was Beth's recollection of what you got for Mother's Day!"

Another brilliant moment. We just had to make sure that we were able to piece together all that Beth took in as her life moved forward.

## The Year Is 1994

My career in journalism came to a sudden and unexpected halt in 1988 as news editor of a 50,000-circulation daily when I received a strong career change offer into public relations by a company that would eventually be bought out by Sprint. Five years after joining the Sprint family, our Bristol operation was teaming up with four other companies to become one large regional entity in Wake Forest, North Carolina.

Off we headed as a family to Raleigh for a new adventure with essentially a brand-new but very complex child entering an unknown school system in Wake County. Beth's first year at Millbrook Elementary School was a disaster! Inclusion was the goal, but Beth was teamed with a one-on-one assistant who was legally blind; the pair was placed in the rear of the classroom, where the assistant struggled to see the blackboard. Beth was isolated from classmates, and we had many tearful Individual Education Program meetings to try to right the Titanic for our daughter!

In the end, we held the upper hand and, with my wife as a special education teacher, we knew the rules that mattered most. The administration visited the classroom, acknowledged our concerns - the lack of Beth's interaction with students and activities - and off she headed to Underwood Elementary School in downtown Raleigh.

A new teacher, a new assistant and a new atmosphere in 1994 looked promising. It was accentuated by my visit to the classroom, where I was asked to introduce Beth to her new friends and explain to them the reality of what they would witness in their interactions with her. I recall encouraging them to work beyond the obvious to get through to Beth and engage her in all that they did in the classroom and beyond!

Her new friends quickly developed their own effective yes-no communication system with Beth. It was a hand-squeeze system; one squeeze for yes, two for no. And they began to get to know her well. She said yes to joining them for their coastal ecology elective that year, which meant a trip to Atlantic Beach for a two-day adventure dissecting squid, hunting for sea squirts in the salt march, and taking a challenge course in the woods!

Five weeks into the school year, this class earned a pizza skating party at the local rink. Beth wasn't going to miss this fun, despite her latest state of incapacitation. A week earlier, she'd gone under the knife for the chance to walk again. She had surgery to extend her tight hamstrings and heel cords so that she could perhaps walk with assistance following her four-week hospitalization in 1991, when she lost her ability to walk independently. She was in full-legged casts in her wheelchair and needed a posse of protection at the rink.

That support showed up in the form of 30 friends when Beth, younger sister Katie, and I pulled into the skating rink parking lot. There must have been a sentinel on watch for our arrival. A stream of those 30 classmates came running to the van to greet us and whisked Beth away in her chair for an evening of bonding and fun. I remained close by Beth's side throughout the evening in case any health issues surfaced, but for the most part, she was in the spotlight, the center of attention. Friends talked to her, laughed with her and protected her legs from any accidental bumps. These fifth graders were soaking up her authenticity.

At one point, four of her friends rolled her to a table and taught her how to play poker!

Just before the party came to a close, the skating rink director surprised me with an announcement encouraging the skaters to clear the rink. He wanted Beth to have a chance to experience a moment of glory, and asked her sister and a friend to begin wheeling her around the rink.

His plan was perfection, heart-warming, emotional. As Katie and Jerrod each took a wheelchair handle and started her on her journey, the lights were lowered, and the rink director began spinning the hanging mirrored ball, creating the swirling circle of lights.

I was in a corner of the room, looking on from afar when I heard applause starting to grow. It grew louder - and Beth broke into a big, appreciative grin!

And then the director stuck an emotional dagger in my heart by cranking up Mariah Carey's song, "Hero."

A miracle moment of the grandest of inclusive opportunities for our daughter had just unfolded. Another bountiful blessing was handed to us on a silver platter. Life was swirling skyward. I lost my breath again!

―――――――――――――

Beth's mesmerizing life was something I simply couldn't hold to myself; I had to share it with my telecommunications colleagues at Sprint, who too were struck by what a unique life Cindy and I were experiencing.

Regulatory director Larry Bays had the responsibility of bringing the five companies to a place of similar goals with a single voice and mission. And in 1994, the first year our companies joined as one at a new headquarters in Wake Forest, we weren't "getting it." Larry had to bring the 600 employees together for a week of team building activities to establish a new face to our company and create a fire in the hearts of every employee to continue being a national leader in the telecom industry.

Larry planned on bringing in a national motivational speaker to rev up the staff. It turned out to be Michael McKinley, president of the National Speakers Association that year, a veteran speaker, someone who can move audiences to live a stronger life.

But Larry didn't stop there. He knocked on my office cubicle one day and sat down with me to share his admiration for our complex and inspiring journey with Beth. Then he popped the big request: Would you share this journey with your fellow employees; would you talk about how you and Cindy continue to make important adaptations as you discover more about your daughter; would you identify how you push the envelope each and every day to ensure that both you and she have quality in your daily living?

Larry, this will have to be very personal if I am to have an impact on the lives of my colleagues, I explained. Give it your best shot, he said.

I began to relive the dozen years of chaos and exhilaration we had spent bringing the life of daughter Beth to this point of importance. It was a huge compliment to Cindy and me to share our whirling dervish of a story with the Sprint family. Cindy and I were 37 at the time and had been asked to travel a strange and unknown journey as parents that few if any in the audience would have traveled. Would they get it? And would I be able to summarize this climb up Mount Everest effectively enough to motivate this team to perform?

The team-building day arrived, and I had my story well-prepared. I had pulled out all stops. I had laid my heart and soul on the line. And then I found out that I would be following the president of the National Speakers Association. He was delivering his motivational message just before lunch; I would open up the afternoon with my story titled, "In All Her Silence."

His story was strong and entertaining, and it drew a big round of applause. My story, laced with fear, fright, joy and fight, drew a standing ovation from my colleagues. I really couldn't believe what I was witnessing. The lump in my throat was huge!

And it was topped off by a conversation with Michael McKinley, who came to me and told me that this story - one that filled his heart with inspiration - was one that I should take on the speaking circuit across America. He said it would motivate people to live their lives in a much more meaningful way; it would elevate their perspective on life and its true relevance. He said my story could move any audience at any level.

Nineteen years later, I have been honored to have shared this story – and the ensuing years that led to Beth achieving her own kind of greatness in life – to tens of thousands of people at conferences in places like Seaside, Oregon, Salt Lake City, Ottawa, Boston, Asheville, Atlanta, Miami, Albuquerque, St. Louis, Knoxville, Raleigh, Washington, D.C., Seattle and many towns and cities in between.

Larry Bays, you triggered an awfully important opportunity without ever anticipating what a powerful end result it would produce!

The Year Is 1995

Megan was a classmate you'd never remember. Until she became unforgettable to us the night after the pizza skating party in downtown Raleigh.

She was a quiet fifth grader - almost to a fault. She wore a cute smile every time we crossed her path, but she stayed in the background, shy and demure. If asked, you might identify her as the least likely classmate in a fifth-grade classroom to reach out and touch the life of a kid with disabilities. What we learned was that she had no close rival when it came to this thing called love.

Megan's impact on our world was most profound that Friday afternoon when Beth arrived home from school. As always, our first course of action was to check Beth's fashionable book bag to see what kind of day she had from her daily journal.

That meant digesting a fairly lengthy note of some detail from her one-on-one assistant about her morning class schedule, student interaction, her lunch, an afternoon of classes, and any scattered anecdotal activity at school that might be worth mentioning. There was always something fun and a bit unusual happening at Underwood Elementary School because the kids themselves didn't hesitate to interject their personality into the classroom to spice things up.

Often times, Beth's notebook contained tidbits of commentary from students about Beth's fashionable taste in clothing, her hair style that day - punctuated by some fancy bow - or the hand-squeeze communication mode shared exclusively by her and her classmates.

On this particular Friday in late September, with school already five weeks in session, we anticipated some extraordinary commentary in the daily journal about the Thursday night party.

And it was all there.

But there was something else in Beth's bag, an envelope with "Mr. and Mrs. Timp" written neatly across the front. Cindy opened it, and then smiled.

Mr. and Mrs. Timp,

My name is Megan Hall and I would like to see if you would let Beth come to my house on Saturday and play.

Sincerely,

Megan

Simple but poignant! Powerful! The first invitation Beth had ever received from a friend, and she was now 12 years old.

Saturday morning arrived, and by 9 a.m., Beth and I were at Megan's home, sharing our joy with Megan's mother that Beth had such a meaningful impact on her daughter. There were plenty of health issues I had to share with Mrs. Hall - including the potential for a grand mal seizure - but even that most frightening of episodes wasn't going to deny Beth this moment of supreme significance.

Throughout the year, Megan and Beth teamed up as best fifth-grade friends, a daisy and a rose, simplicity and complexity sharing special moments that they would likely hold in their hearts forever.

The year evolved into one of our daughter's best ever. And it ended on a falsetto crescendo when Beth was named the Spotlight on Students award winner at Underwood Elementary. This honor was given to the single biggest "over-achiever" at the school.

Beth had cleared every hurdle, was everyone's friend, worked hard as a dedicated student. And when she received her plaque one evening at the school board office, she separated her hands on her own, placed her award in her lap, and clapped appropriately for every single student from all the other schools in the Raleigh/Wake County school system who won their Spotlight award.

Beth's eyes were wide, her smile wider! Her teacher shared excerpts from an essay she wrote about Beth's value to her classmates, which won Beth the top prize. The words meant more to me than anything else in life:

"Beth is truly an inspiration to all the students and staff members who encounter her working hard each day at school. She is really part of the process," her teacher read. "Her classmates say she is a great friend because she never puts anyone down and she's the best secret keeper around!

"My class is truly special this year because Beth has taught us how to value diversity, be a caring community, work hard at incredibly difficult tasks, and how to truly love one another."

Cindy and I went home that night beaming. Our little mystery of a child - before hitting age 13 and still without a diagnosis - was a bastion of purity in our very complex world. Breath? Gone yet again!

The Year Is 1996

In a very indirect way, Mr. Bays also triggered a diagnosis for Beth by prompting me to tell my story publicly.

A trip to Albuquerque, New Mexico, in March of 1996 marked the moment I first heard the words "Rett Syndrome," and they came from an attorney from Winston Salem, North Carolina.

I delivered "In All Her Silence" as a breakout session in a small conference room at a big hotel at the International Parent to Parent Conference. Twenty-five attendees picked my session, including Pete Clary, who came to me after I wrapped things up and told me he was very moved by Beth's story. But he wondered why I had made no mention of "Rett Syndrome."

"Your video clip clearly showed me your daughter has Rett Syndrome," Pete said. "There is no doubt about it. You don't know anything about this disorder? I can share it with you because my daughter, Petesie, is 10 years younger than Beth and she has Rett Syndrome."

I was obviously stunned that we might be receiving a diagnosis from someone outside the medical world 14 years into our daughter's life, but I was completely impressed with his passion and desire to get us locked in with a world involving thousands of girls who did indeed look and act exactly like Beth.

We began to explore the ins and outs of this neuromuscular disorder. It revealed itself to be our Beth through and through. Yes, she lost the ability to talk. Yes, she lost her motor skills. Yes, she had multiple seizures, and yes, her spine was experiencing a scoliosis twist that might impact her respiratory issues down the road. She had poor circulation in her feet; they were always cold. She had breathing dysfunctions; She would hold her breath for short periods of time and would often blow "raspberries" through her lips. She also had poor sleep patterns, awakening frequently during the night. We would hear her humming through the monitor at our bedside stand; I shared with Cindy that I thought she was sharing some special moments with her friends, the angels.

And, of course, the hands locked together, limiting functional use.

All of this, every single anomaly, truly spoke Rett Syndrome.

But before we could even take Pete's "pedestrian diagnosis" back to the University of North Carolina Memorial Hospital to our neurologist for a life-changing discussion, Pete had contacted the founder of the International Rett Syndrome Association in Clinton, Maryland, to see if I could deliver "In All Her Silence" as the opening keynote presentation at the May 25 annual conference in Boston, Massachusetts.

This was Beth's 14th birthday, a day when we would learn what the long-term future of Beth's life would hold. But I was going to showcase our life story to 350 parents who had daughters already diagnosed with this disorder? And to a team of Rett medical experts, including Dr. Alan Percy, the foremost Rett neurologist in the country, and Dr. Daniel Glaze, the seizure specialist at the Baylor College of Medicine who cared for numerous Rett patients.

Pete Clary knew this team would be present, and he wanted confirmation of this diagnosis for Beth. Cindy and I hauled a very thick folder of Beth's medical past with us to Boston for these experts to examine after my presentation.

"In all her silence, Beth has truly taught me more about the value of human life than anyone else I know," I shared with the crowd. It was a watershed moment for Cindy and me, because we not only received a confirmed diagnosis, but we established ourselves as fighters in the Rett network of experts. We let them know we would share this story to create greater awareness nationally about this complex disorder.

We would join people like actress Julia Roberts to push for financial support for research to find a cause and cure for Rett Syndrome. Beth Timp was one of approximately 2,500 girls and women in the United States with this diagnosis in 1996. We finally had a "family" to join up with and to help us understand what this journey was all about ... and where it was taking us.

Son Joseph should have been overwhelmed by the scene. Strangers dancing all around him, faces he didn't know, young and old, many with a different look to their eyes, smiling, reaching out to him to join them on the disco dance floor.

"Go for it, son," I yelled out. "Have all the fun you want!"

And so he did.

He cut the best rug I'd ever seen from a seven year old. He held hands, twisted and turned, grinned and hugged. He was completely absorbed in this wonderful mix of humanity.

Meanwhile, 31-year-old Christopher Burke, a young man with Down syndrome who played the popular and inspiring character Corky Thatcher in the ABC television series *Life Goes On* from 1989 to 1993, rocked the banquet room with his four-piece folk band. Joe and John DeMasi were slamming on their guitars, singing their popular hit song, "Celebrate!"

I had Beth on the dance floor, hugging her tight, taking small side-to-side dance steps, and allowing her to keep up with the rhythm. She had her arms wrapped tightly around me so that she could reconnect her hands, a very necessary piece of the syndrome that challenged her.

Eleven-year-old Katie was sharing time with her mom. She craved this kind of entertaining atmosphere and had Cindy bouncing around the dance floor with her.

The night was young and our family was sharing fun with members of the North Carolina ARC, or Association for Retarded Citizens, at the Downtown Marriott. The next morning, I'd be sharing my compelling story of Beth's journey of triumph over tragedy as a motivational presentation at the state disabilities conference.

We extended our fun late into the evening. The friendships that our young children were establishing were energizing to them, and they wanted to stay until Corky sang his last note. And so we did.

We fell in bed with such satisfaction. We'd just spent a memorable evening with strangers who became our friends because their world hinged on the love they spread to - and gathered from - others. Better yet, our three children had experienced this strong sense of love - and they thrived in that atmosphere.

Joseph showed that much the following week as he and I were finishing our breakfast back home. In a few minutes, the bus would pull up to the end of the driveway on Colesbury Road, and he would hustle off to school.

Before that happened, however, he had an important question he wanted to pose to me. It stemmed from his perspective on the weekend trip across the state to Winston-Salem.

"Hey, Dad," he croaked, his voice raspy from a weekend of fun. "Does Bethie have Down syndrome or Up syndrome?"

Oh, that question came out of nowhere. I chuckled pretty hard. My son was obviously paying very close attention to what we experienced at the ARC conference. In fact, we'd received Beth's Rett diagnosis only a few months before this visit to Winston-Salem. Still trying to wrap our heads around it, Cindy and I hadn't even shared this "new" news with our youngest child.

"Well, son. That's a great question," I said, looking him directly in his eyes. "Beth actually has Rett syndrome. And Corky, you know, the singer we met Friday night at the party? He has Down syndrome.

"And if anyone has Up syndrome, Joseph, well, I think it's you!"

---

On Beth's 14th birthday, I was on a stage delivering a keynote address to a crowd of 350 parents at a conference in Boston, Massachusetts. The date was May 25, 1996.

I expected that the story I would tell this group was the exact journey they were living, but 14 years into life with Beth, we had no real diagnosis. Was it truly Rett syndrome? A complex, rare disorder that just keeps driving its victim downward. It takes their voice. It takes their legs. It throws all degrees of neurological twists and turns at the victim. It creates tight muscles and poor circulation. The list of complications goes on forever.

Let's go straight to the definition of this ugly diagnosis: "Rett syndrome, a brain disorder affecting development in childhood, has been identified almost exclusively in females. RS results in severe movement and communication problems following apparently normal development for the first six months of life. The characteristic features include loss of speech and purposeful hand use, occurrence of repetitive hand movements, abnormal walking, abnormal breathing and slowing in the rate of head growth. Current treatment for girls with RS includes physical and occupational therapy, and medication for seizures."

And then the words that froze us: "No cure for Rett syndrome is known."

While on stage in Boston as I revealed who my daughter is through a four-minute videotape, the mother of the first child diagnosed with Rett syndrome in the United States - in 1984, two years after our Beth was born - leaned over and "confirmed" that Beth indeed has this onslaught of overwhelming disabilities.

The medical experts in Rett syndrome, in the audience that morning, later met with Cindy and me and nailed down the diagnosis. Atypical but yes, Rett syndrome.

Ok, so where does this now take us? We now understood all of the disastrous effects of this complex syndrome. Does it change how we approach opportunities for our daughter? Not in the least.

Our perspective. We knew more of the difficulties facing Beth in the future; but this wouldn't change our desire to make her life huge, to give it pizzazz and compassion and quality and just so much love that she would spread that love to everyone she could and affect lives in every aspect of her perfect little life!

———————————

"In All Her Silence" hit its peak at a medium security prison in Butner, North Carolina, in the fall of 1996.

A friend of mine at Sprint was so moved by my story that she shared it with her husband, a correctional officer at the Butner Federal Correctional Complex. He believed this story might have some impact on the white-collar criminals at this facility, which had two medium security prisons, a medical facility and a minimum security prison.

I knew of no one famous at Butner when I received my invitation to speak at the prison. Nor would I have been told who was there. But looking back now, there may have been a big name or two sitting in that small room when I spoke of my daughter's unbelievable journey in life and how perfect she was in all her imperfections. Her life was the ultimate reversal of how these prisoners had played out their own lives in such a sad and pathetic way when given every opportunity to succeed. It was a moment of irony at its pinnacle.

Over the course of time, I learned that this prison became quite the collection of white collar criminals, almost a who's who of fraudsters and scam artists. It was the very place that would eventually house convicted swindler Bernie Madoff from New York City. It was his own son who reported securities fraud against Madoff in 2009. Madoff pleaded guilty to 11 counts of felony security fraud and was sentenced to 150 years in prison - and it happened to be in Butner, N.C.

Other inmates landing at Butner included Adelphia Communications founder John Rigas, 84, and his son, Timothy, 53, who were both found guilty in 2004 of securities fraud. Former Rite Aid Corporation Vice Chairman Franklin C. Brown is serving his 10-year sentence in one of the medium-security facility at Butner. Al Parish, a former economist at Charleston Southern University pleaded guilty in 2007 to running what prosecutors alleged was a Ponzi scheme that defrauded investors of $66 million.

And Jonathan Pollard, a former Navy officer, entered a plea deal in 1987 after admitting to spying for Israel. He was eventually transferred to Butner's medium-security facility and is eligible for release in 2015. He may have been in the audience of a dozen prisoners when I arrived on that April afternoon.

I still hear that harsh, cold clang of the prison door closing behind me when I entered the Butner prison. Would there ever be an escape? It wouldn't happen through that door.

I was a confident speaker and didn't really fear this upcoming moment. I was confident this story would impact their lives, or at least leave them with significant regrets on how they'd lived theirs. But I loved having Beth with me because she inspired me to deliver my very best. Her presence always left a huge impression on any audience - and who knows what it would have done to the lives of these prisoners if they could both hear about and see her in person. She might have been scared. Most likely, she would have been bold and daring, looking at these men with a smile on her face, convincing them that anything in life is possible if you stay on the right track. But rules kept her from attending.

I delivered my best performance ever at Butner - about my innocent child, my stoic wife, our medical trauma, our educational miracles, our communication breakthroughs and our love for God - to a party of guilty criminals. This was the year we finally got Beth's diagnosis. We were learning how to make her life rich and rewarding. It wasn't peaking yet, but I told these men in orange that we were confident we could continue moving the mountain in her life.

The ultimate beauty of this speaking opportunity reached its climax when Beth received a touching letter from one of the prisoners a week after my visit that described her life's impact on him. It was filled with grammatical mistakes and misspelled words - but even as an editor, I had no issues with any of that because there was no doubt through that letter that our story had moved him to a better, stronger place in life.

---

"Phil Timp's words during our Rett syndrome family conference spoke to me. I was moved almost beyond words by the story of their precious child, Beth, and their family's journey of despair and emotional recovery upon discovery of Beth's diagnosis of Rett syndrome. Their family's strength, faith and commitment to each other, even during the darkest of times, are an inspiration in the truest of senses. Beth is a true hero and Phil is her mouthpiece." - Jane Lane, nurse, Rett Syndrome Clinic, University of Alabama-Birmingham.

Given this kind of strong endorsement, I had no reason not to speak everywhere I could about our roller--coaster journey with Beth and all that she was teaching us about life!

Since her diagnosis in 1996, I ramped up my speaking opportunities and spread the word in a number of cities and towns across the Southeast and at a few major conferences nationwide.

This hell-to-heaven story was taking off. It was 1998, and the meet-and-greet after I spoke was affecting me in a powerful and emotional way. I met family upon family struggling to live through what we had experienced over the course of 16 years with Beth. I looked into the teary eyes of young fathers and mothers after they heard our story of hope. Their kids were bent and breaking; diagnoses were frightening, their futures were so unknown. And their words of my story's impact on their perception of life going forward that day were equally motivating to allow Cindy and me to continue moving the mountain we were forced to climb.

Could we possibly impact them beyond this story? I tried to be a fundraiser for Rett Syndrome. When I spoke, I encouraged listeners to give and give and give to the International Rett Syndrome Association to help girls with this disorder. But I wasn't getting anything from anyone to assist IRSA.

And then it hit me. If we establish a foundation of our own named in our daughter's honor, we might have a chance to raise funds and give to those in need. Cindy and I discussed this idea and brought it forward on our own.

The Beth Foundation, a 501(c)3, was established in 1998, with a mission of providing financial assistance to families who have children with rare or severe disabilities. We focused on "rare or severe" because many of the more common disorders have strong financial backing.

Disorders like Rett, Batten, Klinefelter or Trisomy 18 don't have a huge population base, and thus, have a limited awareness, which, in turn, limits the funding sources.

With the help of family support to finance the start of our non-profit organization, we established a pool of $25,000 that we've maintained and used over the past 15 years to help dozens of families struggling to overcome financial hurdles.

We helped a California family design a special bed for an overanxious daughter with Rett Syndrome. We gave a gift of a mortgage payment to a mother in North Carolina whose 10-month-old daughter was severely burned in her playpen and lost both legs and an arm; they needed immediate help to maintain their home. We helped several children with therapeutic riding classes; we assisted a Massachusetts family build a sun room so their daughter could enjoy a look at the real world!

We don't approve every request we get; we try to help those families and their children who are reaching that tipping point; we try to turn survive into thrive for as many as we can.

We didn't stop there, however. We used The Beth Foundation as a chance to give to research efforts to help find a cause and cure for this complex disorder.

And then 1999 arrived, and the Baylor College of Medicine had a huge announcement to share with the Rett world.

Dr. Huda Zoghbi, professor of neuroscience, pediatrics, molecular and human genetics, and neurology at Baylor had worked 16 years trying to solve the complexities of the gene in the X chromosome affecting girls with Rett Syndrome at an early age. Most have a reversal in areas of language, motor skills and functional hand use beginning anywhere from ages six months to 18 months when this gene goes off course. In short, it is supposed to shut down the production of protein in the genes around it. When it doesn't, an overproduction of protein creates chaos and confusion in the brain. And as the disorder progresses, balance and behavior are affected.

Zoghbi identified the defective gene as MECP2. A mutation in the gene is often the cause of the disorder. A $1,000 blood test can confirm a diagnosis of Rett Syndrome, and blood samples from other family members can be screened for the mutation, but it is rare that the disorder is inherited because the mutation occurs at random.

This news was comforting for the child-bearing future of our younger children, Katie and Joseph. And interestingly, our own Beth, a child with virtually every Rett anomaly, did not test positive for the defective MECP2 gene - among the 5% who come out clean.

That made no real difference to us, however. Beth clearly was overwhelmed by all that Rett threw at her, and we had to remain her strongest advocates to help her continue to achieve her own kind of greatness in life.

### The Year Is 1997

The phone rang on a Saturday morning when there
was an unusual energy in the house. Snow was falling outside
and snow rarely fell in Raleigh, North Carolina. Katie, 12, and
Joseph, 7, were already outside dancing in the white stuff and
catching big, soft flakes on their tongues.

"Hello?" I answered the ring on the kitchen phone. A
kid's voice - one with a lot of pep and some sophistication - was
on the other end of the line.

"Uh, Mr. Timp? This is David. I was a friend of your
daughter in fifth grade. You know, Beth?" I chuckled to myself.
Oh, how well I do know her!

"You probably don't remember me but I, uh, got to
know Beth real well at Underwood. David. We had a great time
at Atlantic Beach, you know, in our coastal ecology class?"

An odd time for a call like this, from a young man who
was now in seventh grade.

"Go on," I said.

"Well, I had a friend over last night. Jeremy. We started
thinking back to fifth grade and thought about Beth. We
thought she was pretty cool. And we just wanted to know how
she was doing."

Then it hit me! David - the kid who had the uncanny
ability to mix intellect and cool at such an early age. The same
kid who tried to teach Beth how to play poker at the Raleigh
pizza skating party. It was a night that awakened me to the
possibility that our daughter, as complex as anyone could be,
could fit in just about anywhere - if the right peers were on
hand to guide her!

"Wow, David, yes, I do remember you." My throat
caught for a second as my mind raced back two years to the

most memorable - and improbable - year of success at all levels for Beth.

Needless to say, this was an exceptional class of kids who befriended Beth in every way that year. It was an important year of transition for our fragile daughter. She was an import - from another school in another part of town where a kid with multiple disabilities wasn't an easy or proper fit. Beth's "inclusive classroom experience" was about isolation, perhaps to protect her. In the end, that arrangement was her ticket to failure.

The students at Underwood took Beth at face value - bent and broken but trying. They decided she wasn't going to be a spectator at school. These fifth-graders at Underwood Elementary were giving our kid a ride she might not ever experience again. They were making Beth relevant. They were decidedly convinced that she was handi-capable.

She was going to be one of Underwood's classroom leaders, a kid who would pull the others along with the help of friends like David, this kid who was on the line with me.

And Beth appeared to be loving every moment of this watershed year of new friendships and unprecedented acceptance.

"David, Beth is doing pretty well, but I think she really misses you guys," I said. "You gave her a great year. She hasn't had one quite that special since."

"Well, Jeremy and I had an idea," David continued. "We were wondering if we could see Beth. I know it's snowing and all, but we'd like to see her, see how she's doing." I glanced out the bay window in the kitchen into the back yard. The snow was still falling hard and fast.

"David, Beth's up and rolling this morning, but we don't have much of a vehicle for this kind of weather." I knew the streets weren't getting salted. "Tell you what, let me discuss your proposition with Beth's mom and I'll be right back with you. I'm going to make it work if at all possible, David. This kind of offer doesn't come along every day for Beth. Hold on a sec."

I hollered upstairs at Cindy, who was straightening up Beth's bedroom.

"Gotta run something by you, hon," I started, as she appeared at the top of the staircase.

"What about this snow," she beamed. I could tell by her expression that she missed her mountains back in Virginia.

"Uh, speaking of the snow, do you mind if Beth and I take a little drive out in it?" I asked. "There's a friend of Beth's on the phone. You remember a David in her class at Underwood. Two years ago?

"Anyways, he and one of his friends want to visit with Beth. They're asking me if I'd bring her by."

Cindy stopped in her tracks, and a transformational look spread across her cheerful face. It was a look of both surprise and parental pride. Her expression gave me the answer I hoped for.

With Beth, we can't carve out these moments. They come at us as surprises, at the most unexpected of times and require us to make an immediate decision before we have a chance to really weigh the potential consequences.

"Help me bundle Beth up," I said. "I've gotta tell David we're on the way."

I hurried back to the kitchen. "David, hey, we're on the way. Just have to find out what part of town you live in."

The directions were easy, but the weather wasn't. Cindy and I quickly wrapped Beth - all 35 pounds of her – into her pink winter coat and pulled a little toboggan cap over her ears.

"How about her feet?" Cindy asked. "We've got to double sock her or she'll freeze."

"Right, but we won't be able to get her shoes on," I answered. "No problem. I'll carry her in and out. I just need to get going."

"Bethie, we're off to see a couple of your old Underwood friends, David and Jeremy," I told her as we stepped outside onto the driveway and walked gingerly to the car. I kissed her after strapping her into her seatbelt. She was awake and alert, apparently fully in tune with this adventure.

As a kid, I was familiar with Wisconsin's extended snows. As an adult, I had weathered more than my share of the frigid winters that slammed the Appalachian Mountains in western Virginia. This wet, white powder in Raleigh didn't rank with what I was used to. The difference was the lack of attention to the roads - no salt, no scraping, no Carolina work crews anywhere in sight. And so the snow created a safety hazard that I wasn't going to ignore or take lightly. I had precious cargo on board our minivan.

We made our way across town with careful determination. Yes, we slipped and slid a time or two but I would never reveal those scary moments to Cindy.

Thirty-five minutes later, we pulled into a cul-de-sac in David's neighborhood and spotted our destination. David and Jeremy were visible on the front stoop of a handsome two-story colonial style home. Obviously eager to see their friend, they were outside waiting for us and tumbled down the steps to get to the car in a hurry.

I would have to be Beth's mouthpiece; I know David and Jeremy knew that. What I hoped for - and what was completely unpredictable and out of my control - was how engaged and interactive Beth might be during this visit. It was my dream for the day to have her take full advantage of this friendly invite. I wasn't disappointed.

A gracious host, David invited us to have a seat in the den. He didn't need prodding from his parents to make this happen. It was obvious to me that he and Jeremy - two seventh grade boys - were behind this idea 110 percent.

I sat Beth down in an oversized chair and started removing her coat. Both boys offered to help, so I let them. Then they settled in front of us and began firing questions at me to get an update on this teenage girl they obviously ranked high on their list of former classmates.

Our visit lasted an hour and a half, and Beth absorbed every moment as if it were her last. She was alive, alert and happy, her head following the conversation like a spectator at a tennis match.

When I finished updating life with Beth, it was David's turn, then Jeremy's. They hit the highlights was eager animation. They were award-winning story tellers, acting out scenes from middle school- their ultimate goal? Keep Beth fully entertained.

Beth, meanwhile, was buying into every word. Her tiny hands were busy during the course of our entire visit, as if she was using them to keep up with the quick pace of conversation.

"You remember the great time we had at Emerald Isle?" David piped up. "I remember digging Beth's hands in the squid when we dissected them. Beth, you remember how weird that felt? And we wandered all over the island on that challenge course. You remember how we pulled you out of your wheelchair and made you do every single thing we did?"

Then it was Jeremy's turn to reflect.

"I remember when Beth won the top student award at Underwood - what was it called? The spotlight award, I think." Jeremy beamed.

"Yeah, that was one of the best nights I ever had," I chimed in. "I'm glad you brought that up, Jeremy. It was neat what your teacher said about Beth that night. She said Beth was a great friend because she never put anyone down and she was the best secret keeper around!"

We all laughed.

And in no time, our visiting time was up. The snow had accumulated substantially during our 90-minute time of story telling. And we bid our warmest farewell to two boys whom we'd never see again but who left an indelible impression on us.

As for their impact on Beth? I placed her in the front passenger car seat and buckled her in tight. And as I climbed into the driver's seat, I glanced to my right and down at her. It was at that moment that she delivered the defining moment to that Saturday morning.

Her angel eyes locked onto my face, expressing complete and utter joy for what she had just experienced. Together, we had created another profound memory together. In that one moment, this Saturday snowstorm had been transformed into a winter wonderland.

Beth followed up that look of love with a grin of gratitude.

"You're welcome, Beth." I returned the look of love.

She then dropped her chin to her chest, closed her eyes, and fell into a deep sleep, fully trusting that somehow I'd navigate our way home safe and sound. She had given it her all!

---

When I married Cindy Prince, I expanded my family experience in a really big way. I picked up people who would play different and important roles in my life along the way.

Seven years after losing my father, I would gain a significant mentor in John Prince, a role model father who had walked away from an alcohol addiction years ago when most of his children were in their preteen years. He had grown up in a coal mining camp called Stonega, raised pigs to help his family survive the Great Depression, had joined the Navy at age 15, came back home to work in a coal mine for only half a day before eventually going on to dental school in Richmond, Virginia, and practicing dentistry up through age 86!

Phil and his father in-law, John Prince, take living all too seriously!

As a replacement father, I leaned on him time and again, as his daughter and I confronted countless hurdles in this thing called life.

Cindy's mother, Phyllis Prince, became a second mom to me, and I eventually became the "son of her heart" as life unfolded for her daughter and me in a most unexpected manner.

Phyllis also grew up in the Appalachian Mountains in a town called Honaker. That speaks to her toughness. She was a stay-at-home mom, with a ton of responsibility in raising five sons and a daughter. Just when I began dating Cindy as a junior in high school, Phyllis suffered a brain aneurysm that should have taken her life. She showed herself to be a woman who handled crises with great stoicism. It was she who never gave up on her husband's alcohol abuse at a time when her six children needed both mother and dad. She kept the family a tight-knit unit despite the daily duress. Without knowing it, she was preparing them for a period of time when they wouldn't have her at the helm to run this ship.

It was the summer of 1974 when her hemorrhage nearly took her life, and Phyllis was only 42 years old. A brain bleed of this magnitude required a lengthy recovery, and she was out of pocket as the leader of this family for up to several years. Cindy, at age 17, had to take on this role to at least her two youngest brothers, Phillip and Jeffrey, who were 12 and 9 respectively.

This dedication and love for family was the single greatest characteristic that stood out to me over time and created that spark in my heart for this woman.

Then there were the five brothers whom I came to know and respect greatly at so many different levels. Each was a graduate of Virginia Tech, showcasing that idea of following family tradition.

The oldest, Marty, became a pulmonologist. Steve also got his medical degree, in internal medicine with a specialty in sports medicine. Bill went into construction, joined a company in the mid-80s in Bristol and turned it in the right direction to a huge extent. Today, he runs that company and owns a good portion of it.

Phillip found his niche in the food service industry, stayed put in his hometown, and ran a series of different locally owned restaurants. He and I were running and cycling partners, strong competitors and very close friends.

Jeffrey, the youngest, after getting his master's in institutional advancement at Vanderbilt University, became a principle fundraiser for colleges and universities in the Southeast, the most significant at Emory University in Atlanta, with most of his time spent seeking financial support from Emory alumni in the Big Apple. His latest venture is at Davidson College in North Carolina, where he lives with partner Michael Jolly, an entrepreneurial artist.

The Prince family is a four generation family of love and support in the face of any monstrous challenge.

Long before these professions played out, we got to know each other on a family fun level by spending time in the woods with bows and arrows as deer hunters, though I never saw a single buck and, thus, never had to harm that innocent Bambi. We were weekend warriors, playing football in the backyard bowl. We played poker on Saturday nights, shared time camping at the beach, and had loads of conversations around the kitchen table while downing home cooked meals. The "farm" was the ultimate weekend destination, a piece of land occupied by a few horses and a bull named "Balls," who created countless memories of chaos and fear for this family, including the time when Balls charged the fence where John was standing and had his nose pierced with a pitchfork to stop him in his tracks!

As life evolved and Beth entered the picture as the second born child among this large family, we would learn how extraordinarily fortunate Cindy and I were to have two brother doctors by our side to "figure things out" when Beth hit another bump in the road. They brought their expertise to her bedside in a significant way at her 1991 four-week hospital crisis and helped pull her through.

Then there was a 1997 episode when these two men ultimately saved our daughter's life once again, this time in Chapel Hill, North Carolina. Beth was 15 and her little spine was twisted and bent at a 60 degree curve. Her thin little body was leaning hard to the right. Severe scoliosis and kyphosis - or rounding of the shoulders - were the newest gnawing issues for us.

If these debilitating issues continued to worsen, and they would, Beth's breathing would eventually be significantly impacted. She would develop respiratory distress and frequent pneumonias that would take her life.

We had no choice but to prepare for a complicated operation that would require a set of rods installed on both sides of her spine to straighten it. The surgeon would do a spinal fusion, which would stabilize and reduce the size of Beth's curve and stop the curve from worsening by permanently joining her vertebrae into a solid mass of bone using screws and wire attached to the rods.

After 13 months in a scoliosis brace to ensure that Beth's spine had pretty much reached its growth limit, we arrived at UNC-Memorial Hospital for this operation. Our daughter would have 18 inches of her back opened up. Reconstructive surgery would take hours. We were nervous.

Brothers Marty and Steve were both aware that we were undergoing this risky procedure and were on alert in case we needed them to help us with any post-operative issues, including a probable pneumonia because she wouldn't move air in and out of her lungs.

Unfortunately, we did.

The surgical procedure went well; we were hopeful we had knocked down any consistent respiratory trouble and would have Beth with us for years to come.

Day three of recovery arrived in the ICU, and Beth woke up early with a red-hot forehead and a 103 degree temperature. I was with her, giving Cindy a chance to catch up on her sleep. She didn't get to. When the nurse notified me of her fever, we reached out to Marty and Steve. What's going on? Pneumonia was the answer from both. Get a chest film done now.

I tracked down the nurse and encouraged her to get this going. She tried. And then she ran into a brick wall in the form of a resident physician who refused to order an x-ray for Beth. After continuous prodding and pleading, we finally got a visit from this resistant resident doc.

He had an obvious and disappointing "I'm the doctor, you're the patient" kind of attitude, telling me Beth just wasn't in any danger at this point. He'd wait a day or two to see how she faired.

I stepped up and demanded that he follow our request. "My brother-in-law knows Beth well, he's a pulmonologist, and he insists that we get this done now!" I said.

"I'll get one ordered," the resident said, "but I won't look at the results until this evening."

And he was gone.

We jumped on the phone to Marty, then Steve to share our concerns. "We'll make something happen," they said.

Five hours later, in the late afternoon hours that day, Marty and Steve showed up at UNC-Memorial Hospital to get things right for their suffering niece. We didn't know they were coming to Chapel Hill. But we couldn't have been more delighted or relieved, as we remained in "no man's land" regarding Beth's health status.

Marty and Steve requested a meeting, through Cindy and me, with the surgeon who had operated on Beth. They fed us questions; we fired those questions to the surgeon for answers.

The big question: What were the results of that morning x-ray on Beth's lungs? The surgeon did not hesitate to get an answer for us. He contacted the resident who had resisted our request earlier that day and told him to get an answer on what the chest film showed.

Moments later, the answer came back "negative." Are you sure, the surgeon asked him. "Yes, it is clear."

We were all stumped. Why the fever? It had to be lung related, Marty said. We headed to bed wondering why the mystery.

I was sound asleep in Beth's room at 1 o'clock in the morning when the surgeon shook my shoulder and asked me to wake up.

"Beth has pneumonia on both lungs," he said. "I'm starting her on some antibiotics."

My question, obviously, was: How do you know this?

"The resident read the x-ray that was taken when Beth was admitted before surgery. It obviously was clear. I'm not happy. She has pneumonia, but we'll get it cured."

He did. But I can't imagine that surgeon recommended that resident to any practice he respected.

As an addendum to this sad experience, I witnessed yet another weakness in that resident's profile. A few days later, the surgeon visited Beth's room with a group of med students and "the infamous resident" to show them our daughter's lengthy scoliosis incision and replace the oversized band aid covering the cut.

I was in a corner of the room, watching this procedure and keeping my eye on the resident. The surgeon had removed the new band aid from its large wrapper and was ready to replace the old one. He stopped to listen to Beth's lung function through his stethoscope, and when he did so, the resident picked up the wrapper and began wadding it up, creating a crinkling sound so loud that the surgeon couldn't hear a thing.

"Excuse me," he said, his glare a definite lesson learned for every student in the room - and, hopefully, the resident himself!

------

You'll never read anything more stunning, more miraculous!

Among the many stories I heard from parents, therapists, educators and medical personnel once we arrived in the world of this complex disorder known as Rett, none came even close to comparing with a miracle moment for a mother named Claudia from Seattle.

This story confirmed all of the amazing breakthroughs we had experienced with daughter Beth. When a child is trapped inside her body and can't break through layers of disability on a daily basis - and then has a wow moment that drops mom to her knees in complete disbelief, how do you measure the whole of life in that moment? What does it say about a Rett girl's cognitive ability? Is life 99-plus percent daily confusion and constant struggle - with an once-in-a-lifetime breakthrough that redefines all of life for this one individual?

Claudia's daughter - like almost every child with Rett - didn't speak. Never did. Never even said "mama" like our daughter did.

Then Claudia's daughter turned 21 years old. And she "celebrated" the arrival of age 21 with an earth-shattering moment. The story was shared this way.

Every morning, Claudia and daughter Stacey had a ritual. Mom would arrive early in Stacey's bedroom and help her daughter get up out of bed. The two would walk slowly down a long hallway to the kitchen for breakfast. On their way to the kitchen, mom would balance daughter from behind to assist her in her walk.

At the end of the hallway hung a picture of Jesus Christ. Claudia's daughter never failed to stop at the end of the hallway. Was she pausing to make the turn to the kitchen? Or was that pause her show of respect to that figure on the wall? Claudia was never certain, but she truly was always touched by that special moment.

One morning - during that 21st year of life - Stacey changed things up more than just a little during that journey to the breakfast table.

Off they went, down the hall to make the turn into the kitchen. Stacey's stop was predictable. What happened next wasn't.

"Stacey stopped, looked up at the picture, and said, 'That's my Jesus,'" her mother gasped! "I could not believe what I heard! Could not! I jumped in front of her and fell to my knees and asked her what she just said!

"And she repeated exactly what I heard the first time. She said, 'That's my Jesus.'"

Three words in 21 years. And she hasn't spoken since. Did she ever need to?

The Year Is 1998

"Mom, dad, come here! Look who I heard from!" Daughter Katie was excited about something that would be a curiosity to her parents.

The CEO of the Shania Twain Fan Club had emailed our 12 year old daughter from Australia. The message: "Katie, I was so moved by the letter you wrote about your sister, Beth, that I hand delivered it to Shania and she wants to meet Beth!"

"Katie, what is that about?" her mother asked. "How does Shania Twain know about Beth?"

Katie couldn't wait to share her secret cyberspace letter of request on behalf of her special sister.

"You know how much Beth loves Shania's music," Katie said. "I just wrote a letter to the fan club about what Beth couldn't do. She can't talk, she can't walk. But we know she loves Shania and her music! I wanted to make sure she could meet her!"

Passion from a 12-year-old in 1998, when the evolution of the World Wide Web was happening - and she was feeling it out and trying to take full advantage of it!

Cindy and I appreciated this extraordinary outreach. Did we expect anything to play out? Most likely not. A cybernet hoax? Who knows? But we certainly agreed with Katie's appraisal of Beth's love for this country music singer. Honestly, we were hooked on Shania's upbeat attitude. Her music was rising to the top of the country music charts. "Man, I Feel Like A Woman" had us dancing! "Still The One" - one of the best '90's love songs!

No reason not to answer "Ronnie" back. It was only 1998, and "catfishing" didn't exist yet. Tuiasosopo hadn't tricked Te'o yet.

So Katie sent an innocent note back to this gentleman, who fired a note back a few weeks later, informing us that Shania was ready to head out on her first concert tour and that he would find a venue close enough to Raleigh to thrill Beth and our family with concert tickets!

We knew about this rising country star's life story, and it was inspiring. She was the second oldest of five children and grew up in Ontario, Canada. She was raised by an adoptive Indian father and her mother, Sharon. Music was plentiful, food was not in this struggling household. Shania played with a house band beginning at age 8, lost her parents at age 21 in a car accident, and raised her three younger brothers until they were old enough to tackle life on their own. Their sister headed to Nashville, married a rock producer named Mutt Lange, and her music peaked the year Beth Timp got the chance to see her three times in concert!

A five-time Grammy Award winner, Shania was making her way across Canada on tour when Katie received the ultimate surprise from Ronnie that the Timps had tickets to her upcoming concert August 14 outside Washington, D.C.

It was one hot evening when we arrived at the outdoor amphitheater in D.C. for Shania's sold-out concert. I had a copy of my cassette recording of "In All Her Silence" for Beth to share with Shania, and we'd grabbed a red rose as a thank you present. Katie found a souvenir stand on our way in and spent her $10 on four different photos of this country superstar. Her goal: get them signed. Joseph, at age 7, wouldn't stop talking about his plan to invite Shania out to dinner with us after the concert. We insisted that was his responsibility to make that happen.

We settled into a deck waiting area outside, with the late afternoon temperature climbing into the low 90s. I remember fanning Beth to keep her comfortable but far from cool; we didn't want this heat to trigger seizures and rob her of a lifetime highlight. Patience, learned from Beth, became our focus as time passed slowly. We were covered in perspiration when the sun finally set and it was time to meet Shania Twain.

One problem had arisen. Make that two. Two busloads of radio concert ticket winners had arrived to meet Shania along with us. Our "moment" was being watered down, especially when the director of this event notified the newly formed crowd that we had to move quickly in our visit with Shania and not ask for autographs.

"Let's go last," I suggested to Cindy. "This is too important for Beth to have it be rushed. We've got the wheelchair. Let's use that to our advantage."

The "Beth" card! Time to use it! And so we did.

As we entered the celebrity room, Beth was out ahead of us, our beacon of light wearing a big smile! But before we even reached the meeting area, there was a rush of people toward us! It was Shania herself - dressed in a lavender mesh top and black spandex pants - and her entourage, hurrying to greet Beth!

Shania dropped down to greet our daughter eye-to-eye and told Beth she was excited to finally meet her. She shared with us that she'd heard so much about her. The greeting was fast and furious! In fact, we don't remember introducing Joseph at all. Cindy and I were trying to outtalk each other, to share our highlight moments about why Beth loved this star singer and how she communicated all this to us. Katie was bouncing beside us.

Then came the moment of truth for Beth, her opportunity to share a piece of communication with Shania. On her wheelchair tray was a red "big mac" switch that could deliver a recorded message - but Beth had to hit that switch. That means she had to separate her hands to deliver that message.

How could she? We didn't have the five to seven minutes in this meeting with Shania Twain to allow Beth the time to fight to get her hands apart on her own and hit that switch. The start of the concert was right around the corner.

"She's got something she wants to say to you on that switch, Shania," Cindy said. "But we're not sure she'll be able to get her hands apart to share it." And then Cindy hit the "moment of magic." She gently touched Beth's left elbow, and Beth's hands flew apart and she pounded her left hand on that big mac switch repeatedly.

"Shania, this is a dream come true for me, and I love you!" That was the message - through Cindy's voice and Beth's heart - to Shania Twain.

This superstar teared up. We teared up! And Beth continued pounding that message on the switch!

Then Katie nudged me, and whispered, "Dad, you've got my souvenir pictures. Do you think Shania will sign them?"

Our visit was over but I couldn't let this slip by. I was known to "break the rules" and today's rule was "no autographs!"

"Shania, Katie has your pictures in this folder and she wants to know if you'd sign them," I ventured forward.

"Of course, I will," Shania beamed. She asked for a sharpie, and then began signing those 8 x 10s. Problem was, she signed the first two "To Beth, Love Shania!" I had to interrupt her and remind her that Katie needed at least one signed over to her!

Done!

---

The concert opened with pyrotechnics going off on stage and Shania let 'er rip with "Man, I Feel Like a Woman!" The crowd was on its feet, creating an immediate issue with Beth. She couldn't see, the crowd was loud, lights were flashing - and she went into panic mode. Dark, loud places created anxiety for our daughter. She was confused and began crying out. How do we fix this?

I hoisted her 85-pounds up on my right shoulder to get her above the rockin' crowd in front of us, but that didn't matter. She kept moving her head back and forth and uttering cries of anxiety and emotion.

And then Shania herself turned this completely around for her new friend, Beth Timp. She sat down on the edge of the stage, took her guitar, and began singing "... you're still the one I run to, the one that I belong to..."

The crowd took its seat as Shania's sweet voice hit the mark with our daughter. Beth stopped moaning. She stopped thrashing. And she locked her eyes on the stage toward her hero.

Her complex disorder - this Rett thing that was troubling her - was, for one moment, on a path toward normalcy. Shania and she were connected. Beth did not take her eyes off the center of the stage - for the remainder of that song and for the rest of the concert!

She was one happy teenager, soaking up the absolute best in country music from the Entertainer of the Year!

And her sister made all this happen.

I wanted something special and most appropriate to close my motivational message to the education and disabilities world. I needed a legacy song, a sonnet that would speak to both the perfections and the imperfections of daughter Beth and where our journey has taken us with her.

I wanted this piece to highlight our struggles, and then turn to our much greater realization of all she's taught us. I wanted this number to close with the earth-to-eternity conclusion that would bring an audience to its feet. Most of all, I wanted "Heaven In Her Eyes" to be a piercing and defining perspective for every set of ears that heard it.

Pepper Choplin got it done for me. Pepper? Yes, funny, really comical. Choplin - pianist, performer, a name that has famous musician legacy written all over it. Comedic musician? Yes, he is, but he's so much more.

Here's a guy who is my age and has a successful career as a music minister at a church in Raleigh, North Carolina. When we joined his church, he was married and had two young daughters. He could write music so well that Shawnee Press practically owned his every masterpiece. He'd written more than 200 anthems and was so versatile that he could honestly classify his talents as ranging from church musician to theme park entertainer, with musical styles from rock to classical to bluegrass. He was the kind of guy who led events as composer, conductor, clinician and comedian!

Pepper was a guy whose looks reminded me of the slapstick comedian Jim Carrey. He wore that crazed expression on his long narrow face. His eyebrows jumped up and down and his mouth broke into a big, wide grin when he threw his face into crazy contortions. And some of his music matched this.

One evening after choir practice, I approached Pepper in the parking lot outside church and asked him if he would be interested in taking on a different and unique writing assignment. He respected Beth deeply and recognized that this was an important responsibility he needed to say yes to. Pepper liked challenges; his only real question to me at that moment was this: what does Beth mean to you, what does she stand for?

Obviously, Pepper was looking for the theme for this song. That was not a tough question for me. "You know, when I look at her, I really see only one thing, Pepper. I see heaven in her eyes," was my answer.

Two weeks later, Pepper invited me over to his house to share a very sweet and important piece of music that immediately struck my soul. He wanted me to sit down with him and finish the lyrics. I couldn't be more excited with the flow of this special piece, how it opened with the perfect child we thought we had, how it moved to the struggles she and we faced, how it then evolved into my one-on-one conversation with God and my understanding of where her important life would ultimately take me!

Pepper built an important modulation moment in this song. He told me he didn't want to make it too Disney-like. But he did want it to escalate in a powerful way so that the listener's life would be greatly uplifted when hearing this song.

Little did Pepper or I know the eventual impact this song would have on the lives of many - and the author of this piece.

## Heaven In Her Eyes

They placed her in my arms at the moment of her birth
    She was the most perfect thing I'd ever seen on earth.
And I smiled when she opened her tiny eyes to see;
    And I felt a touch from heaven when my daughter looked at
        me.

I saw heaven in her eyes, things I'd never seen;
    And though she never spoke a word my child was teaching

me.

She was heaven-sent, so it comes as no surprise;
    When I look at her, I see heaven in her eyes.


The doctors brought us news that would steal away our dreams
    They said our precious child was not as perfect as she
        seemed.
And they told how she would struggle, all the things she'd never
        do;
    And with every passing day we saw their words were
        coming true.


I cried to God for answers through a long and sleepless night;
    I tossed and turned in agony until the morning light.
Then I knelt beside her bed and whispered, "Why, God, why?"
    Then she awoke and smiled at me and looked me in the
        eye.

I saw heaven in her eyes, things I'd never seen;

And though she never spoke a word my child was teaching

me.

She was heaven-sent, so it comes as no surprise;

When I look at her, I see heaven in her eyes.


She's taught me to embrace today; I've learned my lessons well.

For tomorrow's just a secret that only time will tell.

So look beyond your troubles, for one day we'll be free.

And life is just a moment before eternity!


I saw heaven in her eyes, things I'd never seen;

And though she never spoke a word my child was teaching

me.

She was heaven-sent, so it comes as no surprise;

When I look at her, I see heaven in her eyes.


She was heaven-sent, so it comes as no surprise;

When I look at Beth, I see heaven in her eyes.


Five years after this song was written - and I had sung it at countless gatherings where I spoke, I received a call from Pepper Choplin about the birth of his newborn daughter, Deanna. Pepper was heavy hearted because there were health issues regarding his third child. There was no confirmed diagnosis, but it was clear their little girl had some developmental disability issues.

"Why didn't we stop at two children," Pepper expressed to me. "Why are we facing this? I don't know how we're going to get through this."

"Heaven In Her Eyes" was my answer to this struggling father. "That song was mine, but it is now yours and mine, Pepper. That song happened for more than one reason. It may be hard to fathom this right now, but Deanna will truly be a bountiful blessing in your life. Her challenging life will help you find in yourself a better, stronger father, husband and overall person. This new dimension in your life, Pepper, will result in an elevated relationship with God, and that relationship will grow far beyond what it is today for you."

Ten years later I had the gift of meeting Deanna during a return visit to Raleigh to deliver my message to my former church. Her diagnosis was cerebral palsy. She was animated, happy and bright. This young lady had already led an effort to have a handicap-accessible playground built in her city.

There was no doubt that she was turning her dad's life into something far more powerful and important than he ever anticipated. I had no doubt that he truly saw "Heaven In Her Eyes!"

## The Year Is 1999

Beth's first year in high school in Raleigh was a grand slam. Yes, major-league baseball great Josh Hamilton was indeed part of her story.

Hamilton's tale of baseball stardom is well documented. He made his major league debut in 2007 with the Cincinnati Reds as an outfielder. He was an All-Star in his rookie season, and then was traded to the Texas Rangers. In 2008, Hamilton wowed the baseball world with his power, hitting 28 homers - and setting a record - in a single round of the home-run derby at the All-Star Game at old Yankee Stadium.

He continued making the All-Star roster the next four years, and in 2010, he peaked as the Most Valuable Player in the majors.

But there is a lot more to the Josh Hamilton story before he even made the big leagues.

Hamilton was a 1999 graduate and a superstar on the baseball diamond at Athens Drive High School, and he knew Beth Timp for one reason. At the end of every school day, Hamilton would swing by Beth's homeroom to pick up a friend of his, Ashley Pittman, a young man with Down syndrome, who was the Jaguars baseball team manager.

This baseball star was 6 feet, 4 inches tall and 200 pounds. He ran the 60 in 6.7 seconds. His fastball was clocked at 96 miles per hour. He hit .529 and had 13 homes, 34 RBIs and 20 steals in only 25 games his senior season. He was being scouted by every major league team. He might be a number one pick in the '99 MLB draft.

This kid could have been about himself and only himself. The baseball world had him under a microscope - but he was someone different. He cared about a special needs kid whom he took to the baseball field every day for practice.

The Jaguars lost to a team one afternoon in Greenville, North Carolina, and Hamilton showed his heart to his coaches and teammates. During the post-game meeting in the outfield to discuss what went right and wrong with the game, someone came running up to the meeting to inform the team that manager Ashley Pittman was in the bus crying because the team lost.

Hamilton jumped up from the team meeting, turned to his coach and asked for the opportunity to head quickly to the bus to comfort Ashley.

On the bus, he let his friend know that with baseball, losses can happen and will happen, no matter who's on the team. Ashley's response: "We have Josh Hamilton, we can't lose."

Hamilton ended up being the top pick in the Major League Draft, with a signing bonus of $3.96 million. He made sure Ashley Pittman got a bat signed by all of the Tampa Bay Devil Rays after he threw out the first pitch at a Tampa Bay game after signing with the team.

And he made sure he signed a baseball for one of Ashley friends, Beth Timp!

But Josh Hamilton's dream went south very unexpectedly after his first year of minor league ball and being named Minor

League Player of the Year in 2000. He and his parents, who had sold their house in Raleigh to follow his dream career, were in an accident in Orlando, Florida. Hamilton's back was injured. In recovery, he became hooked on drugs and alcohol. He tried recovery at rehabilitation centers but failed to turn his life around.

His major league team, the Tampa Bay Devil Rays, sent him to the Betty Ford Center for drug rehab, but he failed a 2003 drug test, showed up late for practices, and eventually was fined for violating the MLB's drug policy. He was not the player - or the person - he was at Athens Drive High School. And no one expected his baseball journey to take this route.

Meanwhile, Beth's autographed baseball remained on her dresser. We knew nothing of Josh Hamilton's troubles. He'd just disappeared from any baseball lineup - for three years.

Businessman Michael Chadwick and minor league manager Roy Silver are credited with turning Hamilton's life around in 2006. He had to literally work his way back up the ladder of respect. Hamilton cleaned bathrooms and raked the infield at Silver's baseball academy. He eventually married Chadwick's daughter, Katie.

And then he found God. And he found life again. Today, as a new outfielder for the L.A. Angels, he knows he is never cleared from his former addictions, but he continues crediting God with his successes.

And Beth's baseball? It remains a special keepsake in a life filled with special moments.

## The Year Is 2000

I didn't know the turn of a new century would welcome us with such a profound learning experience called extraordinary parental courage.

We met the McSpadden family in the vestibule of our church one Sunday morning in Raleigh. They happened to show up as guests on the morning I was sharing my life story about Beth. As it tends to do, the story drew plenty of tears. And my role as guest speaker had me shaking hands and dishing out hugs with my wife and three children at the back of the sanctuary. It was always an emotionally draining but powerfully rewarding experience.

Then the McSpaddens stepped up to introduce themselves.

And the connection was made, immediate and life-lasting!

Les was more, a gentle monster of a man with a loving expression. He held his oldest son in his arms. The little boy they introduced him as Jaime - wore a pair of thick glasses and a happy expression. He didn't say a word, but he was clearly a reflection of his father's loving persona

Wife Annette was tiny beside her husband. Her black eyes were shimmering, her cheeks tear stained. She was smiling through all her pain. She held an infant in her arms, another baby boy, this one named Nicholas.

Between them stood their daughter of maybe 8 or 9 years of age. Katie was tall and thin and had mom's black eyes. She wore a shy smile as we oohed and ahhed over her bright, shining face and the close resemblance to her mother.

Fate had them at Greystone that morning. They were in the early stages of some devastating years ahead. Their three-year-old was slipping away from them, going downhill pretty quickly. A mitochondrial disorder was leading to lost vision and motor skills. Jaime didn't talk. But he smiled incessantly, giving us a positive to comment on in the face of what we were quickly recognizing as a story even more challenging than our own.

That they would be in the congregation that morning - the one morning I told our church congregation about our compelling journey of life with Beth - was a reason to believe that friendships aren't always just happenstance. Sometimes they are carefully orchestrated by a higher power for an exact purpose!

Sharing a journey of purpose-filled pain with other parents experiencing a similar journey is powerful. Sharing that journey with parents who must endure the loss of not one but two little boys in a three-year span is cataclysmic. It is, without a doubt, life changing.

In a matter of moments, we knew we were going to be challenged with a new role to play - a strong, unwavering role of supporter, when we'd spent the first 18 years of life being the needy ones, the ones who were reaching out to others to ask for their help in guiding us through a life of parenting that didn't have a book of guidelines to follow.

---

Delivering a eulogy honoring the life of a four and a half year old boy is almost beyond words. But words are exactly what I needed as I stood in the sanctuary of our church in Raleigh on March 2 with the casket of Jaime McSpadden only a few feet from me.

It was easily one of the most powerfully raw moments of my life. Three years later, on July 28, 2003, the pain would intensify when I had to repeat this eulogy experience but replace the name Jaime with younger brother Nicholas McSpadden.

Not once but twice within a gut-wrenching, three-year span of life, the subject of childhood death stared down the parents of these little boys. Les and Annette McSpadden had been caught in the cruelest of downward spirals that slowly drained life from their two boys. These brave parents exhibited characteristics in parents I have yet to witness in anyone else.

In the wake of the deaths of these two little brothers who didn't make it to five years of age, I was asked - and honored - to tell their stories in God's house before their brokenhearted loved ones.

Bridging life to death somehow came much easier than I thought it would. Maybe it was the joys of life that these little boys shared with family and friends that kept creasing my mind as I worked hard to write the very best accounts of their innocent lives.

This is what I shared on March 2, 2000, to a church filled with hurting souls for the life of one small boy. I opened with this song:

### One Small Boy

One small boy taught us how to love each other
One small boy showed each one of us such joy.
One small boy made us question God's existence, but it was in his persistence,
that God lives with us today ... in one small boy.

One small boy - thanks for sharing with us, Jaime.

One small boy - thanks for showing us the way.

One small boy - thanks for bringing us together, holding hands
with one another,

praying for just one more day ... with one small boy.


One small boy - made us laugh and cry together.

One small boy - made our hearts soar with his smile.

One small boy - made us look into the future; now we know
that our forever

is secure in God's great hand ...

in one small boy ... in one small boy ... our one small boy.


Thirteen century poet Rubi wrote: *"You've seen or heard of goats going down to the river. The lame and dreamy goat brings up the rear. There are worried faces about that one. But look, now they're all laughing because as they turn to head home, that one is the leader. Learn from the lame goat ... and lead the herd home."*

What have we learned from our little leader, this one small boy? What has Jaime McSpadden taught us about life? Why don't we start with the greatest of these - love?

This one small boy taught us how to express love to each other.

Love nourishes, comforts, strengthens, sustains.

Love creates invisible lines of connection.

Love begets miracles.

This one small boy taught mom and dad - and the rest of us - about unconditional love, that kind of love in which we are willing to give and give and give again, and expect nothing in return.

But oh, did we get something in return! Did we ever benefit from this gift of love from Jaime Manuel McSpadden.

Jaime's life reinforced the passage in Jeremiah 31:3 - When the Lord appeared to Jeremiah and said: "Yea, I have loved you with an everlasting love." Jaime brought out in all of us the ability to develop an everlasting love for one small boy.

I believe Jaime's life really called forth the best in those who knew him best. His life is a poignant reminder of what is eternal, of what abides after everything else is gone.

In so many ways, Jaime forced us to live a better kind of life, didn't he? He made us realize right from the beginning that the very best part of the book is where? On the inside, after we open the cover!

He helped every single one of us become better people instead of bitter people because of the grace and beautiful purpose in this one small boy.

Jaime's life inspired all of us to think of what's most important in life. He stripped away all the masks that we like to wear and exposed all the little games we play. His life was pure and straightforward and simple.

No airs - no put-ons.

Certainly, that defines life at Frankie Lemmon School, where Jaime spent some of the very best days of his life. Tuesday, I had the wonderful opportunity to visit this preschool. It was a school established in downtown Raleigh in the 1960s for children with disabilities, and it was abundantly clear to me as I visited classrooms and spoke with parents and teachers why Jaime McSpadden thrived in this environment.

It was all about friendships! Profound friendships Jaime made with the delightful band of very special children attending this school. Communication barriers disappeared here! Kids connected at any and all levels. And that made Jaime McSpadden feel like he belonged.

In fact, this one small boy not only belonged, but he was "The Man" when he arrived at school! He was king of this castle! His personality bubbled over while at Frankie Lemmon - unless, of course, head honcho Janet Sellers showed up!

The joy on his face as he made his way down the hallway toward his classroom each morning is a memory that will never fade for Director and Principal Martha Lee Ellis. That grin was irrepressible. Physically and socially, Jaime thrived at Frankie Lemmon. It was all about quality of life, Ms. Ellis said, and Jaime was finding a big dose of it there.

Jaime's first teacher at Frankie Lemmon, Nancy Johnston, told me that Jaime's parents were painstakingly careful to work all kinds of separation anxiety goals into his education plan to make the transition smooth for their son. Are you kidding? As soon as Jaime spotted Caramy and Damon and Sarah and the rest of the gang, he never looked back - probably much to mom and dad's chagrin!

Kids almost fought each other to get close to Jaime. Why? Because his reaction each and every time a classmate interacted with him was one of appreciation. It was as if he was saying, "Thanks for believing in me. Thanks for making me belong."

It was their opportunity to assist, to give, to share. Would most of us fight each other over the opportunity to help another individual? Lesson learned.

Ms. Johnston shared that Jaime was also very musically inclined. He would charge in his walker toward the CD player when his favorite Barney music began playing, and he'd begin his own dance - weight shifting from one foot to the other - and he'd start singing his song: "Yah, Yah, Yah, Yah!"

His independence was also something to behold! One day he took off from the classroom without his walker and began crawling - under supervision - out the classroom door, down the long hall to a set of steps, and up those steps to get to the outdoors, a favorite hangout of Jaime's.

He would also toss puzzle pieces in the floor, and then throw his head back in laughter, defying anyone to make him pick them up! Mom wanted the staff to be tough, but sometimes they just had to laugh with Jaime.

His influence was profound even when he wasn't present for a classroom activity or field trip. When Kelly Grant, Jaime's teacher this year, took the kids on a field trip to a duck farm, Jaime wasn't up to going. But Kelly and classmates wanted to honor him by taking part in one of his favorite activities, feeding goldfish to the ducks! But Kelly, in the rush of preparing for the trip, forgot her box of goldfish. Now I said earlier that love begets miracles? Just so happened that one of the parents happened to have her own box of goldfish in her car, and so she saved the day!

The wonderful memories go on and on. But one that must be told is the very special boy-girl relationship between Jaime and Caramy Peebles. Caramy, you see, was Jaime's girlfriend, hands down.

And as mom - Hunter Peebles - tells it, it was a very stereotypical guy/girl thing because Caramy would wait on Jaime hand and foot - and, as is the man's way, Jaime would let her!

She is one little girl who could always prompt a laugh from Jaime, even on his toughest days. When told of Jaime's passing earlier this week and his flight to heaven, Caramy told her mom: "Then I want to go to heaven, too!"

Jaime's struggles forced us to ask the hard questions about life, didn't they? His persistence to overcome incredible odds time and time again kept his parents alternately jumping through hoops and standing on their heads.

Love begets miracles? I know they ended up getting medications for Jaime that heretofore were impossible to get.

And so what is the ultimate reward for his parents and for those of us who have watched this one small boy live this kind of life? I turn to a line sung by Jean Val Jean in my favorite Broadway musical, Les Miserables: "It's when you love another person that you see the face of God."

Les and Annette, how often have you seen the face of God during these trying months?

Now, I'm going to gush a little about Mom and Dad here. And I hope they'll forgive me later.

Like magnets, we are drawn to people and places that will complete us in some special way. That's Les and Annette McSpadden.

Les and Annette, like it or not, the power and grace of the Jaime story didn't happen without you. We all stood by and watched in wonder as this story of incredible faith and deep abiding love of parents to child unfolded.

Your grace, your spirit, your endurance were tested - over and over again. Any wonder that your little boy had the staying power that we all marveled at these past few months? His role models were quite exceptional and he simply didn't want to leave this intense relationship behind.

Les, the life of this small boy is very much about the life of a father who toiled with the responsibility of supporting his family the very best he could under such trying circumstances, of being torn between home and work - of sticking it out and earning that graduate degree to make sure his little boy had everything he could possibly want or need in life.

John Gray in the book "Men are from Mars, Women are from Venus" talks about the male as someone who must be able to solve the problem. Otherwise, he is not happy but you took a different approach, Les, realizing that this was not a problem to solve.

Mythologist Joseph Campbell said, "Life is not a problem to be solved, but a mystery to be experienced." Les, I believe you adopted that very perspective.

As things unraveled for your son, as circumstances spun out of your control, it was not your way to panic. You never lost touch with reality; you stood solid, always making the right decision to be there to help hold things together. You've been defined by many as silent and strong. A gentle giant of a man. The exemplary father who always put family first.

I will tell you, though, that we got a good laugh on you Tuesday when I visited Frankie Lemmon School. The story goes that when you and Annette had decided that this was the school for your little boy, it was you - not Annette - who showed up to tell the staff of your intentions, maybe because you are a formidable and perhaps intimidating presence. But your message to Ms. Sellers was this: "My wife, Annette, wants Jaime here!"

And Annette, have you EVER redefined motherhood. The life of this small boy was undeniably about the life of a mother who created a love and commitment so intense it was noticed and admired by all. Unconditional love doesn't even touch it! Any wonder that your little boy chose to stick around and defy the odds?

Former Notre Dame football coach Lou Holtz once said a person's greatness is measured in how they handle adversity. If that's the case, Jaime is a legend - and you two aren't far behind!

Les and Annette, Jaime came into this world all yours. But because of the kind of people you are, generous and giving, you gracefully and politely  - with no trace of bitterness - allowed a world of people into your life with Jaime - and guess what? He became ours, too!

We all grew to know a greater intensity of love because of Jaime. We have all had a chance to get a glimpse of a very unique side of life through Jaime. We certainly understand that life is just a moment before eternity.

We came to appreciate that big open-mouth smile, his head thrown back in total glee, the mischief in his eyes, the squeals of one small boy undaunted by the barriers and imperfections that tried to get in his way.

And Katie and Nicholas - I know that as you grow, Jaime's importance will grow in magnitude. You will be compassionate and caring of others' needs because of the life your brother lived.

I believe you will take all the values that Jaime stood for with you throughout your journey in life.

I love this Indian Proverb: "Where you were born, you cried and the world rejoiced; live your life so that when you die, the world cries and you rejoice." Doesn't that define Jaime's life?

It's we who are crying now, while Jaime rejoices - rejoicing that he had this family of believers in who he was and what he stood for.

And don't you know he's throwing that little head back and laughing now. He's singing his Yah, Yah, Yahs as he races down the hallways in the Kingdom, telling the Master what a very special life he shared with some very special people here on earth.

This one small boy helped me understand that when we are faced with our own mortality, we have to ask the question: "What did I bring to this world that is of value? What is there about my life that is eternal?"

Les and Annette - and friends and family gathered here today - we are a lot closer to answering that question because of Jaime Manual McSpadden. What a legacy - for one small boy.

_____

Unfortunately, that was only round one for Les and Annette McSpadden. Their Nicholas was next. He would peak in his development at two years of age and then begin to regress. His parents found out he, too, was a victim of the same mitochondrial disorder that had taken the life of his older brother. The diagnosis came shortly before Jaime's death, adding an even deeper degree of suffering to all that these parents would experience as they laid to rest their oldest son.

Nicholas had even more fight in him than Jaime had. Maybe he'd witnessed his older brother's struggles and refused to give up easily.

Or maybe his fight was led by parents who refused to go down easy, knowing the exact path this little vulnerable human being would be traveling because they'd lived it all up close and painfully personal already.

Nicholas had "cowboy" in him; the family loved horses, so they transformed that passion to this little boy. Many days were spent at a stable called J&H. It's where Nicholas cut his teeth on horseback riding - and thrilled everyone who came to watch him perform.

In the end, he didn't let go of those reins very easily. I remember his mom and dad mustering every bit of faith and strength to "encourage" him - in a soft whisper - to let go.

Heaven is waiting for you, Nicholas. We can be brave, little cowboy, because we know you are brave. And in their arms in that hospital room, he listened to them - and finally let go.

I remember the call from Annette to our home in the mountains of Virginia, announcing the impending death of son number 2. It was July 2003, a little more than three years since we'd all buried Jaime. We raced to Chapel Hill, North Carolina, praying the whole way for parents who couldn't possibly endure the loss of yet another child.

It was time to start writing again. A repeat from three years ago? No - this was Nicholas, a different kid, a different life. And yet another moment staring me in the face and taking my breath away.

And so on July 28, 2003, I wrote:

### From Boy to Cowboy

A broken little boy took a trip one day
To a ranch where his sister Katie would play.
He'd heard about cowboys and horses and such
I'm not sue he figured he'd fit in too much.

He took it all in, he liked what he saw,

Then this curious city boy stuck out his jaw
And he cracked a big grin and figured he fit.
Soon he straddled a horse with a bridle and bit.

The cowpokes all loved him - he played a big part
He earned their respect and he showed he was smart,
Yes, this boy was a charmer, a bit of a ham.
He even endeared himself to Hilton Lamm.

He earned Hilton's hat and he wore it with pride
The smile said it all - I'm a cowboy, let's ride!
J&H Stables filled the boy's days with fun
He had lassoed their hearts, each and every one!

Little boy, you're a cowboy - you're now free to ride.
It's your turn to gallop with God by your side.
Giddy-up little cowboy, ride tall in that seat
With heaven your home, your journey's complete.

Nicholas Montgomery McSpadden!
What a name, eh? What a beautiful name for a
beautiful boy. It's got kind of an Ivy League ring to it, doesn't
it? Certainly commands attention, doesn't it? There's a lot of
name there, just as there was a lot of boy attached to that name.

Nicholas. A.K.A. Little Man, Nico and Stinky, right,
Janet Sellers? There is so much substance packed into one little
boy.

Have you heard about the wild boat rides he took on the
Sellers' speedboat one weekend and how he nearly jumped into
the wake behind the boat? Oh, yes, Nicolas appreciated the
luxuries of life! Little old Stinky, as you liked to call him, Janet,

nearly got the best of you and his mom on that speedboat, didn't he?

It's a wonderful story and it speaks to the adventurous nature of Nicolas. It all started when the McSpaddens and the Sellers got together for some boating fun one weekend. Turns out that Nicolas discovered his therapeutic playground while on that boat. Janet tells me that he was all over that boat, working his way around the periphery - walking here and there - while she and mother Annette scrambled after him to keep him from walking the plank and tumbling overboard into the lake! Talk about a physical therapy workout!

Then there was the wake kicking up from behind the boat! That held a real fascination with Nicolas. In fact, Janet is certain he would have launched himself into that wake if she and mom hadn't had such a watchful eye on him.

The faster that boat went, the more the wind blew through his thick black hair, the louder that engine roared beneath him - well, the bigger the smile on that young 'un's face! And boy, could he ever express himself with that smile! That long weekend has been described as the best of Nicolas' life because he experienced such unbridled joy while on that boat! He truly had a need for speed! May heaven contain at least one large lake for a little boy who loves riding in a speed boat!

Stinky really became his name because at times, he was just that - a little stink pot! At least to Janet he was. A bit of history is required here. Nicolas was expected to follow older brother Jaime to the Frankie Lemmon School, where Jaime had such great success and was known as "the man" at the school.

Well, little brother had other ideas. Oh, he loved to visit the wonderful faculty at Frankie Lemmon. And he loved to absorb the love that every individual offered up at this special school. But school there? No way, no how!

Yes, Janet Sellers - mean, old Ms. Sellers, as she came to be known to Jaime - was convinced she could play that tough act on Nicolas McSpadden and that he'd just fall right in line! HA! This little man was in charge of his journey, and he was going to manipulate his way right into Janet Sellers' heart! And so he did. She became one big softy - a marshmallow whenever Nicolas paid her a visit.

He'd poke that lower lip out, and mean old Ms. Sellers would say, "Now look, buddy, look Stinky, it ain't going to work that way." But guess again - it always did.

We can all imagine some of the early conversations between brothers Jaime and Nicolas reunited in heaven on Thursday. The conversation may have gone something like this:

Jaime - "Hey, little brother, welcome to the greatest place you'll ever know! Way better even than that speedboat! And how is mean old Ms. Sellers at Frankie Lemmon?"

Nicolas - "Mean, old Ms. Sellers? Listen, she was nothing but a big pushover - you just have to know how to 'work' that old marshmallow!"

Nicolas was plenty spirited and could get mad as a hornet if you didn't give him his way. Ms. Sellers tried it and failed. But he wouldn't hold a grudge. He'd get mad, and then he'd get over it. And he'd allow you to work your way back into his good graces.

I need to mention that Nicolas Montgomery McSpadden was a master manipulator of the heart! Just ask rough, tough Cowboy Hilton Lamm, who heads up J&H Stables, about how a 4-year-old kid can throw a lariat around your heart and reel you in!

The story goes that Mr. Lamm, who is described as an old-school cowboy, has a tough side to him that few can penetrate. Well, one dry, dusty North Carolina day, this little neophyte cowhand by the name of Nicolas McSpadden shows up at J&H Stables to check out the landscape, see what his sister Katie's been up to, see where she's been spendin' all of her time. Well, it wasn't long at all before all kinds of special accommodations are being made for this special little cowpoke. The sky was the limit!

Now, I've learned through this story that one of the cowboy commandments is this: A cowboy shalt not ever, never, not ever share his hat with anyone else. If you're a real cowboy, you just can't allow that tough venire to be cracked. But guess what? Nicolas McSpadden has worn Hilton Lamm's own cowboy hat! That's right, the head of the ranch, Mr. Lamm himself, personally placed his own 10-gallon hat on Nicolas' head - making that young'un a bona-fide cowboy!

Truth be told, I would venture to guess that the entire staff at J&H Stables broke cowboy commandments on a regular daily basis for Nicolas Montgomery McSpadden.

There was also the side of Nicolas that didn't mince words about what he wanted. And with all due respect to the marvelous medical staff at UNC Memorial Hospital who cared for this little boy, he had a way of letting his mom and dad know when he was mad! Often times, that anger did surface - not surprisingly - at the hospital!

Point of fact - during a recent visit to the Pediatric Intensive Care Unit at the hospital in Chapel Hill, Nicolas got mad about something - I mean really mad. Les and Annette describe it as the maddest he's ever been. In fact, his heart rate jumped to 206 beats a minute and he was turning blue because he wasn't allowing himself to breath during this crying jag.

Well, the doctors got concerned, as well they should. They saw a little kid turning blue, obviously not getting enough oxygen, right? But mom - as always - knew best.

Give him a minute, Annette told the medical staff. And sure enough, 60 seconds and one round of itsy-bitsy spider later, Nicolas was back to his old self.

Oh, and did I mention that Nicolas was a master manipulator? Yes, this little boy had the doctors taking off their white medical coats before they entered his room. He had convinced them that the best approach was to lose the clinical look and just be themselves. And it worked. If they forgot, they'd hear from him, loud and clear!

Then there's the story of Santa Claus, a.k.a. Daddy McSpadden. This story has it that Les, in his volunteer spirit, has been Santa Claus the past couple of years at both Governor Morehead, the school Nicolas attended, and Frankie Lemmon, his brother's school.

As I understand it, Nicolas was petrified of Santa Claus when he was three years old - and what three year old isn't? So in order to ease that fear, Santa McSpadden started getting dressed at home in front of his son so that the little guy could get acclimated to the fact that the man behind the suit was the very man he doted on in life - his Daddy! Well, that worked perfectly - until the moment that the big white beard was applied - and then Nicolas fell all apart! Dad could be Santa Dad to a degree, but Nicolas was NOT going to share his daddy in full costume!

In the past few days, I've asked lots of people important to Nicolas to share their recollections of this happy, little boy.

The smile, oh, his smile, gotta be his smile, that smile, the way he smiled. It's locked in our memories. It was a big, open mouth grin, an effervescent smile, a 'what about ME' smile!

Nicolas had a smile that said, "Believe it or not, I'm lovin' this life." A smile that said, "Believe it or not, I'm the one in charge here!" A smile that said, "I'm dictating the pace, I'm setting the standards." A smile that said, "I'm leading you all along, and - like Frank Sinatra - I'm doing it my way."

You never had a doubt how this little boy felt. You never had to guess. His face was so very expressive. When he was in pain, it showed all over his face. When he was joyful, it radiated from deep inside him - and then showed big on his face. And you never doubted who he was - he was a child of God in the purest sense.

Nicolas' ability to express himself, to communicate clearly, despite the fact that he couldn't talk, was not lost on the group of nurses who played such a vital role - especially during those very tough last few weeks at the hospital. They worked so very diligently to ensure that Nicolas had quality of life. They managed his pain in such an acutely focused and caring way to allow for quality of life. We express our deepest gratitude for their care and concern during this most difficult time.

Last Tuesday evening, my wife, Cindy, and I hurried to Raleigh from our home in Virginia, and while on the road, Nicolas took a turn for the worse. When we arrived at UNC Memorial, we got to experience first hand the goodness of this wonderful nursing staff in the three short hours we were there. It is a night Cindy and I will remember forever.

As divine intervention would have it, I came across a quote Saturday that ties me back to that night so perfectly: I don't have the author of this profound statement, but - Les and Annette - it so brilliantly defines the selfless and unconditional love you showed your son - and he showed you - last Tuesday night.

"Life is not measured by the number of breaths we take, but by the moments that take our breath away."

Ironically, as little Nicolas fought for every breath that night, my breath was completely taken away by all that I witnessed.

Les and Annette, you were standing at the foot of the cross that night. Caring for Nicolas that evening was the best of the best - a nurse from Brooklyn , New York, named Diane D'Orsino! What insight from this young woman, what Christ-like qualities she brought to that setting.

She defined Nicolas this way: "His eyes were the windows to his soul. And I saw a soul that was 20 times his age. Nicolas was the little boy and the old soul in one gorgeous little package. The depth of that soul was very present through his eyes. When he looked, he looked deeply; when he smiled, he smiled large."

Ironically, when it came time to die, this little boy did it with Christ-like qualities - with such grace and dignity and respect for those around him. Here was the little boy who had lived life with so much overt expressiveness. He always had mom on her toes because she was never certain where he was leading her in life.

And yet, when it came time for him to die, he loved his parents so much that he allowed them the chance to drift off to sleep on a Wednesday evening, knowing that he could bravely take that next step - and move on to eternity. He was a brave little cowboy to do so.

During our discussion that evening, Diane and I reflected on body and soul. And we kind of figured it out, didn't we, Diane?

We asked ourselves: Why could we see that little boy's soul so clearly through his suffering? Because his little body, in all of its imperfections, was not allowed to mask his soul. It was there for all of us to see. Nothing was getting in the way. The trappings of life don't get in the way of the spirit; they don't mask the truth. A perfect body can distract us from the goodness of the spirit. It often doesn't let the spirit shine through. Nicolas never put on airs, nor did he play games. In short, he wasn't covering up his true self.

In that regard, he also allowed us to all stay present when we were with him. What do I mean by that? When so much of life is lived through society's expectations, we learn to appreciate Nicolas at that moment. But this little boy was expectation-free! We learned to focus on the moment with Nicolas and not look to tomorrow when we might be discouraged with what he might not do.

Nicolas brought us together that Tuesday evening, and through his particular suffering and bravery, we were learning about quality of life in the truest sense. We were witnessing pain management and stoicism and fear and, of course, the sanctity of life - all in the same transformational moment.

During the course of that evening, Diane and Stacy Pardue shared with us their very poignant stories about witnessing death through the passing of their parents; about being unshackled from this physical self and entering God's kingdom; about seeing that realm of angels waiting for us to escort us into heaven.

It was powerful beyond words, what we witnessed that night. I was encouraged not to be afraid. It was all so important and intense and real.

And yet, there was Nicolas on that threshold - and mom and dad were wondering what it was going to feel like this time around.

"Sad awe" is the way Diane D'Orsino described the moment. And yes, there was tremendous sorrow mixed in with all the other emotions.

Robert Williams said, "I know of only one starting place in the war against sorrow, and that is in the arms of Almighty God. In so many ways, Les and Annette and Katie, it has been much more than a skirmish or a scuffle or a battle - this unique set of circumstances you've fought the past eight years. It has been an all-out war as Robert Williams describes it. I can only guess that this has been a kind of Armageddon that you've had to experience.

But God has a higher purpose for his people. He is faithful to use our most painful times to mature us, to draw us into closer dependence on him.

Annette, you put it best one day as you held Nicolas in your arms at the hospital - the deeper the sorrow, the greater the blessing. I see that in you.

I don't know if you realize it or not, but you were Mary at the foot of the cross last week. And you were unfailing in the enormous act of selfless love you were asked to perform. You loved your son so much that you could let him go to be with his Heavenly Father.

Nurses Nicky, Suzanne, Amy, Jamie and Sarah were equally impressed with the McSpadden family. They described you as cool, calm and collected under unbelievable circumstances. They were amazed at your perspective, given the very serious nature of your son's illness. They called you extraordinarily strong people - and you are! You are so deeply respected by family and friends for the grace and dignity you've shown during this journey.

For me, you redefined unconditional love in those powerful moments on that hospital bed at UNC Memorial!

I had to look up the word "awe" because I have been in complete awe of how you have lived life these past eight years. Here's what I found: Awe is defined as a mixed emotion of reverence, respect, dread and wonder - inspired by authority, genius, great beauty, sublimity or might.

I am in awe of you, Les McSpadden. Dad. Nicolas' dad. Do you realize you were idolized by your son? Wow. That all dads could be so honored. I mean he wouldn't even share you as Santa Claus with anyone else. That's something! Janet Sellers said the only place Nicolas was happier other than on that boat was in his Daddy's arms!

Annette - I have to be honest with you, your husband called you a few names the other night - he said you were a very strong woman and a great mom! Somehow, I don't think that's the first time you've heard those compliments, Annette.

Katie, you are a most precious angel to your parents right now. You are treasured by them and by all of us as a young lady who has experienced many, many significant events in life - and you are only 11. It is our prayer now that God will continue to wrap his loving arms around you and protect you throughout your very important life. I wish for you so many successes.

I hope all three of you will allow this congregation of people who love you dearly to provide gentle, insightful care to you in the weeks and months and years to come. It is certainly something we're committed to doing - because you have shared with us so many profound lessons for a lifetime.

Through this experience, we are getting the opportunity to ride the coattails of one Nicolas Montgomery McSpadden into heaven. Personally, he opened the window last Tuesday night enough for me to get a glimpse of heaven. It convinced me that eternity is something I must pursue with everything in me.

Can you imagine what's going on in heaven right now? There's got to be a double-joy of celebration breaking out as the McSpadden brothers are reunited for eternity!

And so, dear Nicolas, this congregation of loving people who have gathered here this morning to pay tribute to your precious and holy life now offer up this prayer:

May the road rise to meet you, may the wind blow at your back, may the sun rise warmly on your face. May the rain fall softly on your fields, and until we meet again - yes until we meet again - may God hold you in the palm of His hand.

Amen.

---

The fall evening was almost a little too balmy, even for the first high school football game of the season at Abingdon High in the western mountains of Virginia. But for two special-needs students who couldn't handle freezing temperatures very well, this was the perfect opportunity for them to sit side-by-side as best friends at a football game for the first time ever.

It was the turn of the 21st century, the year 2000, and the Timps had just moved back to Southwest Virginia from

Raleigh. Beth was in her second year of high school, and lo and behold, a friend from long ago was a new homeroom classmate of hers. His name was Justin Hale, a young man with cerebral palsy who always wore a big smile and a positive attitude.

On the third day of the start of school, Justin went home to inform his dad that Beth Timp was in his class! The bigger news he shared with Danny Hale was that he had a crush on Beth!

This friendship could be tracked all the way back to when they were four and five years old and sat next to each other on the ground at a support group picnic attended by the Timps and the Hales. We still had photographs of Justin leaning to his left to give Beth a kiss on her cheek! The infatuation had an early start in the lives of these two challenged individuals.

We heard word of Justin's "excitement" toward Beth not long after he shared it with his dad. That's when Danny and I touched base to try to create a special moment for these two young high school students. An early-season football game seemed like the perfect opportunity to drive more fun in their lives.

Little did we know *they* would make it the perfect evening for their dads.

We arrived at Falcon Stadium and got Justin and Beth out of our conversion vans and headed up a long hill to the top of the stadium, where we decided to pick them up from their chairs and let them sit side-by-side on the concrete bleachers. Danny and I would serve as "bookends" for Beth and Justin to make sure they were safe and stable.

A warm wind was comforting as we watched the teams warm-up. The smile on Justin's face was huge. Then he surprised us by turning to his dad and asking Danny if the two of them could go to the concession stand and buy Beth a navy blue Falcon football sweatshirt. Of course, his father grinned!

Minutes later, the two arrived back with the last size small sweatshirt available. Danny gently placed Justin beside Beth again, and Justin gently placed the sweatshirt in Beth's lap.

I thanked them on Beth's behalf; my heart was swelling because of Justin's kindness.

The game got under way, and halfway through the first quarter, I saw Justin reach out and touch Beth's forearm. It was obvious he was checking to see if her arm was cool enough to require the warmth of that new sweatshirt he had bought for her. I leaned over and asked him how she felt. He said she was fine.

The game rolled into the second quarter and just before halftime, Justin reached out again to check Beth's comfort status on her arm. "She's still fine," he told me, grinning. We grabbed some hotdogs for Justin and Beth at halftime as dusk turned to dark at Falcon Stadium. Danny and I were thrilled at how special this event was unfolding.

The third quarter "touch" happened as we expected. "Are you sure she's still comfortable," I asked Justin. "She's not too cool?"

"She's still fine," was his answer. The Falcons were hammering their opponent, the crowd was loud, and we were having fun! When Abingdon scored, I would stand Beth up and hold onto her as I cheered on the home team.

The fourth quarter arrived, and so did my favorite "Justin - Beth" moment ever!

Justin reached out for one final check of Beth's comfort status, and then leaned over to let me know that she was "a little cool."

"It's time to put that sweatshirt on her, isn't it, Justin?" I said with total joy!

"Yes!" he answered. His pride was over the top!

I slipped that blue sweatshirt on Beth. She was happy; Justin was overjoyed!

The Falcons won the game, and Justin won over Beth's heart.

And mine.

### The Year Is 2004

The big yellow envelope arrived in Beth's wheelchair backpack on the last day of her best year in high school. It took us by surprise, but the message in large black letters on the envelope didn't. "For Beth, With Love, Second Period Eng. 9 Ch."

The Ch. stood for challenge - appropriate for this class because it was an advanced English class that was pushed to excel. Ironically, Beth also created "challenge" for this class.

My excitement in opening this packet was sky high, and my anticipation was rewarded. The envelope was loaded with hand-written essays - more than 30 of them - written by Beth's classmates as a year-end exam.

The surprise came from teacher Brenda Vernon, an eternal optimist who invited, or rather insisted, that Beth Timp be a member of her class. This woman, who wore a perpetual smile and a positive outlook all over her person, got it when it came to Beth and her powerfully subtle influence on people. There was some motivating factor in her desire to "fit" Beth so seamlessly into her classroom. Maybe she was clairvoyant and knew that disabilities would eventually become personal to her - like when she became a grandmother and gained a grandson with Down syndrome long after Beth left her classroom. There was just a lot of "good" in this lady's DNA.

Brenda was genuine "teacher" through and through. Didn't matter that our kid didn't talk or that she fell asleep in class on far too many days to count. Or that she'd get into an annoying, self-stimulating, rhythmic pattern of blowing "raspberries" with her lips. It just had to have disturbed the class. But Brenda Vernon? She handled Beth's complex classroom behaviors with aplomb. Never a disparaging word was whispered about our daughter. In fact, it was all good all the time.

Brenda's strategy on handling class disturbances was masterful. In fact, she turned them into positives, making certain every single student bought into her upbeat outlook that Beth would surely leave the deepest, most lasting impression of any student in her class.

And to prove it, she gave her students the ultimate test in an English challenge class. Write an essay at the end of the school year that defines what this different and diverse classmate named Beth Timp really meant to you this year.

An assignment like this can bring out the best in students. In my opinion, it gave this group of 30 classmates a little more incentive to close out the year on a high note because they were asked to write about one of their own.

When we opened the yellow envelope and saw page after page of handwritten essays, it was obvious that every student took this assignment to heart. Most of the lined pages were full, telling us that sufficient thought and significant impact were at play in the writing of these pieces.

———————————————

Honestly, what do you think about a high school kid who says this about your daughter: "I think of her as one of those pens that comes as a bonus when you buy a big pack of pencils. It can still write, like she can still communicate, but, like Beth, it just uses different methods of doing so." The kid's name was Tyler. At 14, he was extraordinarily intuitive about what made Beth tick. And I immediately placed him high on my list of exceptional young people!

Maybe he was reflecting on the Romeo and Juliet assignment during the year when Beth showed up with a whole lot of eye gaze answers to questions about which modern-day celebrities would best fill the roles of Capulet, Montague and Benvolio in Shakespeare's epic tragic romance.

"I have learned the skills of patience in having her in my cooperative learning groups - and that will take me forward in the real world," Tyler continued. Who was this kid, I asked myself as I read on:

"Another thing I have learned is to not judge a book by its cover. I will be honest - along with others, I was surprised when I found out Beth was smart. And I was touched when I read her one-act play. Then as the year went by, I saw signs of communication such as a head nod or a leg shake.

"Thanks for being such great parents to Beth. You seem extremely involved and patient with the way Beth communicates."

He won my heart completely and wholly. His brilliant perspective took my breath away!

---

That was only the start of some impressive prose written by youthful minds that experienced Beth in an academic setting - something even we, her parents, could neither confirm nor deny. We accepted their insights and read on in wonderment. It was obvious by what we read that Beth had wowed her peers with convincing responses on her eye-gaze board; she sold them on her legitimacy.

"I didn't realize how well someone with one of her disabled traits could listen and cooperate so well. She has been an inspiration to my life to never stop trying," wrote Hayley.

"Thank you for allowing me to enjoy Beth's company all year long and learn about her and from her," she wrote, addressing her essay to "Beth's family."

Elizabeth had this to say: "I liked how she was the carriage when we acted out scenes from A Tale of Two Cities. Also, she brought in another project that was very interesting and shared it with us."

Laurence was especially thoughtful, writing: "I have learned that no matter what disabilities a person may or may not have, they still are able to have opinions and emotions about certain things. Even though Beth can't express herself the way the other students in the class can, she still finds ways to get her point across. Watching Beth advance through the work assigned to our class within the same amount of time as the rest of us encouraged me to work harder."

The kid then stuck an emotional dagger in my heart, closing out his essay with: "She has offered insight on how a strong family can make a strong person - and Beth is definitely strong."

The diversity of thought and perspective about Beth was fascinating. Lacey wrote that "even though (Beth) is unable to do stuff that normal kids can do, she still sets her goals high and stays active with other kids. She is a very special girl who I think is a great and admirable person."

Kim had a slightly different take on Beth: "I can't look at her without smiling. She just glows in our classroom ... When I see her in the hallways, I always stop and talk a minute with her and Rhonda (Beth's assistant). Beth truly is a wonderful person. I'm sure no one could truthfully say otherwise ... It's been a great year in English."

As far as I'm concerned, these kids were acing this class. Every single one of them!

And so let's continue with Lauren's take on Beth: "...I can tell that she is a very determined person ... that is such a good quality in a person ... Beth has made me a more understanding person."

And Maggie: "I admire her way to do everything to the fullest."

Sarah delved a little deeper in questioning whether she takes too much in life completely for granted: "I never really realized how privileged we all are, but then thinking about it, maybe we're not that privileged at all. I mean, yeah, we're all smart and we're born with everything we need to one day become whatever we want to be, but if it takes someone else to make us realize that, then how privileged could we really be?"

So Sarah, you're asking us all to ponder whether we, in fact, appreciate our many blessings without witnessing the fight in a fragile being like Beth Timp to remind us of how we put life on cruise control far too often and fail to find out what we're really made of. Without a "Beth" before us on a daily basis as a visible reminder to maximize our gifts and talents, we fail to capitalize on our "privileged" status. I'm hoping I did justice to Sarah's message.

Classmate Katharine used some of the most complimentary descriptives of the Beth she came to know and respect. "She always has a positive and upbeat attitude toward life ... having Beth in our English class has not only been a learning and growing experience for her, but also for each of her fellow classmates. Beth has never been anything but a participant throughout the year and that shows dedication. I am privileged and honored that I could share my freshman year with such a wonderful woman."

Heather called Beth "quite an inspiration to me because she has an aura of determination that surrounds her." She defined that determination this way: "When I think that something may be too difficult for me to accomplish, I think of Beth and what she has accomplished under her circumstances. She motivates me to do well ... I can sincerely acknowledge the fact that I have been blessed. Beth has an amazing amount of bravery as well. She seems to make the best out of what she was given, and that is a wonderful, wonderful trait to possess."

Thanks, Heather. My heart is swelling yet again for the depth of character Beth has shared with you all!

Justin took a practical approach in his perspective on Beth: "I have learned that people with disabilities can still be active participants in class. They can be part of your group, share your thoughts and feelings, and even get you out of an answer on a quiz!"

I like the use of the exclamation mark, Justin! More than that, I treasure the thought that Beth worked her magic to affect a quiz question! We didn't know she possessed those powers - or that she'd be conniving enough to put them to work!

"She has taught our class important lessons that we will never forget."

Thanks, Justin. She's taught all of us life-changing lessons!

---

Elizabeth Nicole Timp. Our daughter's name had just been announced as a graduate of Abingdon High School on June 5,

2004. She was 22, yes, 22 years old. For a special needs student, it was time to leave high school. The milestone moment had arrived. It was a standard milestone for millions of high school students. For Beth and others like her, the milestone was a bit more momentous.

This Saturday morning was brilliant and beautiful, highlighted by the Navy blue graduation gowns worn by the 200+ Abingdon high school graduates.

I was on the football field with Beth and her fellow graduates, the only parent not in the stands. I was standing by her wheelchair when her name was announced. But I was not going to escort her to the front of the field to receive her diploma.

That was the responsibility of two of her closest classmates who were seated next to her and were beyond excited about this opportunity! In fact, they had "won" this opportunity, beating out a half-dozen other classmates to be the two key escorts for this special needs graduate.

But it wasn't necessarily a breeze, this escort process; there was a definite high risk factor in her potentially stumbling and even falling on the football field as she made her way to Principal Bo Ketron for the presentation of her diploma.

Cindy and I were willing to take this chance, after having taken risk after risk throughout Beth's school career in the hopes that the chances we took would result in highlight moments in her life and in the lives of those around her. Her Abingdon High School friends had bonded so closely to her that we wanted to close out her career by having them participate in the closing moments of her senior season.

We knew exactly how deep Beth's impact had been on her classmates when they voted her "most respected" in her senior class and best chorus member! Her chorus classmates treasured her friendship to the extent that they would create Shania Twain concerts for her and deliver them to the entire student body. Beth was on stage with them, soaking up every special moment.

Why not let her fellow classmates carry out the one final milestone moment that would probably remain with them the rest of their lives?

I had spent some time with the two classmates who would escort Beth to the front of the football field to get her diploma. I wanted to make sure they were confident in carrying out this process. I carefully showed them how I handled Beth in and out of her wheelchair. I showed them Beth's limited muscle strength, her balance issues, how they should lean her to one side to get her moving forward so that she would begin walking. We practiced together on how to slide Beth gently to the front of her wheelchair and plant her feet firmly on the ground.

There was no doubt this was the highlight of their morning. Would Beth cooperate? When her name was called, her friends moved quickly to get her standing, but their next steps were slow and measured as they began the journey across the football field. It was obvious the crowd in the stands picked up right away on the difference in this graduate's journey to close out her high school career. Within seconds of Beth and her accompanying friends moving forward, the crowd rose to its feet and began a growing applause that lasted a number of minutes.

Beth, decked out in and gown and sporting a gold sash representing her membership into the National Honor Society, met Principal Ketron when the applause reached its peak.

Rett syndrome kept Beth from being able to separate her hands and accept her diploma. The plan was already laid out. One of for friends would hold her steady while the other took her tassel on her graduation cap and moved it to the other side, indicating in every way that Beth Timp had earned her diploma as a high school graduate.

As she turned to head back to her wheelchair, her two friends by her side, she saw that her entire class was standing in deep appreciation of their inspiring classmate and all that she had accomplished, despite the challenges that tried to knock her down.

## The Year Is 2006

On the first of June in 2006, Cindy and I could be portrayed as desperate parents. We were desperate for help for daughter Beth. We did desperately not want to turn over Beth's care to yet another stranger. We'd been burned and burned badly. No, worse than that. In the category of trust, we'd been torched.

That day I arrived home to find a woman we'd entrusted to Beth's care passed out on our recliner in the den, unable to wake up when I called her name repeatedly, left me empty, disappointed beyond measure, lost, frustrated, angry, betrayed - and, yes, desperate.

Beth couldn't defend herself from harm. She couldn't report abuse. She didn't cry out to gain attention, nor did she spend hours crying over any level of negligence. At least we hadn't seen it yet.

If not our worst fear in life, it certainly was a close second to losing Beth to a sudden, unexplained illness. Or her outliving us.

From our parental perspective, Beth had redefined the ability to tolerate pain. She accepts it as part of daily living. But she certainly shouldn't have to accept pain heaped upon her by a negligent caregiver. And yet, how would we ever know? Short of catching someone red-handed, we would never find out because Beth has no way of reporting abuse. She has no expressive language.

We believe she trusts us completely and wholly to surround her with honest, reliable, compassionate and responsible strangers who would spend eight to ten quality hours with her five days a week. They gently dress her in the morning, prepare a hot breakfast for her, and guide her around the house as she walks with careful assistance. They help decide what she wants to do - listen to country music, watch CMT TV or read another Adriana Trigiani or Nicholas Sparks book. They are responsible for bringing important quality to her daily routine.

I'm sure somewhere deep inside her; she believes we want only the best for her. And yet when a betrayal occurs, how empty are we all? And so I forced myself to believe that negligence in the care of our angel child was simply not possible. It would never happen because everyone loves her to the depth that we, her parents, do.

That's why I was confused when I walked through the kitchen into the den, where things were stone-cold silent. Beth was in her floor seat, her hands in her lap. Things didn't feel right as I walked into the room. My blood chilled to a sub-zero level.

"What's going on here," I asked our caregiver incredulously. I didn't curse. I didn't raise my voice - yet. I'm not the type to overreact until I get the full story. We'd been told this woman had a history of an occasional seizure, which was the first thought that crossed my mind when she didn't respond to me. "Have you had a seizure? Are you okay?"

No answer. She was groggy and struggled to sit up.

"I think someone broke into the house and stole Beth's night medicine," the woman stammered.

This made no sense. Our home was isolated. It was off the beaten path and over a hill from any main highway. We never had anyone wandering in our neighborhood. And besides, our three barking dogs weren't going to allow a stranger to wander inside without a protest and, most likely, a scrum.

I repeated her words but in a mocking tone: "Stole Beth's medicine? What are you talking about? I need to know what's been going on here. Sit up and talk to me."

Then it hit me. Beth has been with an irresponsible adult who had taken her who knows where and had done who knows what to her.

The fury began raging in me; as I bent down to get a closer look at Beth. Her face was bright red, as if she'd been exposed to the sun.

"Where have you been today," I asked the woman. "Where has Beth been to get sunburned?"

Beth looked up at me, contorted her face and let out a most uncomfortable cry. If she could only talk, what would she tell me right now?

I dropped to my knees.

"What's going on, Beth?" It was a question I knew would produce no answer. But I had to let her know I cared deeply. "What's wrong, darling?"

Beth's favorite lap blanket was draped across her knees. Her caretaker was sitting up now but still looked confused about where she was and who she was.

And then I made a most shocking and disappointing discovery. I reached out to Beth to lift her up to get her to the bathroom. In doing so, I removed her blanket. Underneath it, on Beth's lap, was lunchmeat, large slices of it scattered all over her lap, a clear indication that the neglect by her caregiver was profound.

I was stunned. Scooping up the dried up meat, I fired out at the befuddled woman who was now leaning over the top of us.

"What kind of day have you put Beth through?"

"Oh, that's where her lunch went," the caretaker said. She chuckled, as if I should be amused at her discovery. I was instead sick to my stomach. "I guess she was trying to feed herself. I didn't know what she did with that lunch meat."

"What are you talking about?" Feed herself? She isn't capable of doing that - certainly not with sandwich meat!

I couldn't ask many more questions. It was time to escort her from the house - with a threat of abuse to set her straight.

How long would it take Beth to heal from this injustice? That was the question racing through my mind as I scrambled to decide what to do next.

And then it dawned on me that it might have been hours since Beth had been to the bathroom. I picked her up gently - all 85 pounds of her - and she stiffened, a look of concern or maybe fears on her face. I carefully sat her on the toilet and stood by to assist her if need be. She rarely needed stabilizing help to balance her, but today was very different. Her hands began shaking, and she started moaning. This young lady had something urgent to share with me, and she was trying. Dear God, she was trying. My angel was a basket case, and I didn't know why!

I leaned over and threw my arms around Beth. I consoled her but she kept shaking. I would never know the truth. But I could remove the horror that caused this nightmarish evening.

After comforting Beth by carrying her to her bedroom and laying her on her bed, I hurried back to the den, where the caregiver was actually on her feet.

"You don't belong here any more," I told her. "What you've done to my daughter is inexcusable. Unfortunately, we'll never know what you did to her today. I don't ever expect to see you or speak to you again."

I then dialed the phone number for her fiancée. "You won't believe what has happened, but you need to come and pick up Leigh. I should file neglect charges against her, but I'd rather not have any other contact with her. She's left us with a completely hopeless sense of trust in anyone with Beth.

"Come and pick her up now, please."

When Leigh was gone, I walked back to Beth's bedroom to check her status. She was quiet and calm. I teared up.

"How can something like this possibly happen to someone so perfect, Beth?"

She hummed softly. The danger in her life had been removed.

I put my face close to hers and told her how sorry I was that she had to endure whatever she experienced that day. Her skin was butter-rich and soft, her eyes forgiving. Fear had left her face. She smiled a smile of trust and love. God's image was all over her.

I sat down on her bed next to her. She was in her favorite fetal position. I suddenly felt much more vulnerable than Beth did.

I pulled my cell phone from my pocket and tried to compose myself as I dialed my wife's number. It was a conversation I dreaded; in moments I would rock Cindy's world with some of the worst news possible, sending her back to some of our most frightening days as young parents when Beth appeared to have no chance to overcome an avalanche of medical problems. This one was different. This one was avoidable - and right now, it felt completely insurmountable.

Each and every day my wife and I revisited the same painful question: Were we ready to pursue another caregiver; were we ready to trust another stranger who shows a composed, mature and compassionate side of herself to us and an advantageous, ugly and deceptive side to Beth. The answer was slow in coming.

Weeks passed with little hope of a solution. Then we heard about a woman who needed a summer job, who was working in a special needs class of high school students, who would be worth at least an interview. It was gut-check time.

Were we in synch with this decision to give it a whirl - or would Cindy and I be in different places where a new caretaker was concerned? Would she ever trust again? Would I become obsessed with Beth's safety while at work, unable to concentrate on the challenging responsibilities of running a public relations firm?

We'd heard good things about Shannon. She was coming from the same school system Beth had graduated from in rural western Virginia, and she came highly recommended by Beth's former assistant, Rhonda, a big-hearted mom who epitomized the soulful character found in many homes throughout Appalachia.

This had to work; our psyche couldn't handle another dishonesty, another betrayal, and another kick in the gut. We had heard that Shannon cared a whole lot for people and their particular plights in life. She wanted children but four pregnancies ended in miscarriages. She had a big heart for the disadvantaged, and, in fact, had partial custody of a young girl with a diagnosis of autism at age 8.

Our interview with Shannon was an immediate comfort to our painful souls. She had an honest face and a pretty smile.

She seemed to be grounded and have a sincere interest in our daughter. Beth watched her closely during her visit to our home.

In the end, it was a lock. Cindy and I shared the same thoughts about her strengths. She wanted to be a good friend to Beth, she herself wanted to take something important away from their relationship, if there was to be one. She wanted to become a better person for having spent time with Beth. And she wanted to reach out and heal whatever it was that had us doubting that we could ever give a stranger unsupervised supervision of our unprotected daughter. Ultimately, she was silently asking us to trust once again.

And so we did.

Parenthood - special parenthood! God help us - now!

---

Shannon arrived at our home on the first of June. She was wide-eyed and appeared eager to please. She wanted to start this summertime relationship on the right foot with Beth, knowing it was a patchwork situation for us and aware that Beth needed something positive to occur in her life. Shannon needed a summer job and would return to her full-time job as an assistant at Abingdon High School in August, when school reconvened.

That would never happen. Beth would make sure of that because her first encounter with Shannon was simply unforgettable. Their first hour together? Well, it was profound.

The two bonded over a plate of pancakes - of all things - at the kitchen table.

As was often the case, I microwaved a stack of three cakes and followed that up by warming up her syrup. It was this plate of pancakes that would be Beth's "proving ground."

I grabbed a chair and pulled up to the right side of the table. Beth was on my left in her wheelchair and Shannon occupied a chair to Beth's left.

I was filled with a nervous energy, wanting everything to fall in place.

Our first course of business was to introduce Shannon to Beth's first love - eating! In fact, food was the single biggest motivation to get Beth to help herself with a task.

So I pulled from a kitchen drawer Beth's adaptive fork, a thick, black plastic handled device that was easy for Beth to grip. In fact, with her limited functional hand use, Beth had a hard time releasing the fork once it fit nicely into her left hand.

I cut her pancakes into small pieces and spread them out on her plate. She looked down at them with an eagerness saved only for her favorite foods.

"Let's give this a try, Beth," I encouraged her. "Show Shannon what you're all about, girl."

I opened her hand up and slid the adaptive fork into her palm.

With my hand on her wrist, I pierced a piece of pancake on the end of the fork. Then I let go and let her take over. Slowly, carefully, Beth brought the fork up to her mouth and raked off the bite of pancake. Without hesitating, she lowered her hand and the fork - and then leaned far to her left in the direction of Shannon. Tilting her head slightly backward, she locked eyes with Shannon.

"See there?" her expression said it all. "Kind of surprised you, didn't I," her eyes spoke volumes.

And then it happened again. And again. And even a fourth time!

The lean and the look stole Shannon's heart. And it melted mine. I wasn't ready for that kind of "special encore performance" by my daughter.

Given all she'd been through with that former caretaker, she apparently decided to take things literally into her own hands and solidify an early relationship with this new caregiver. And so she did.

It wasn't two weeks later that Shannon was locking down a full-time job as Beth's caretaker. Four years later, the relationship had become a mutually respected friendship - so much so that Shannon asked to share her loving perspective about Beth on our non-profit disabilities web site: www.bethfoundation.org.

In Shannon's words:

"As I began my journey with Beth, I was instantly intrigued by her spirit and beautiful smile. She made me feel alive, and I wanted to share everything I could with her. As time has evolved, I have grown to love this wonderful and enchanting young lady, and I feel like I am more than just her caregiver. I feel like a part of her family.

I want her to experience all that I can offer her, and I am more determined every day to make sure that each day she feels loved and safe.

I told her once that she is the only person who sees me for who I truly am and she still gives me that beautiful smile of hers every morning when I walk into her bedroom and say "good morning" to her. That is the most wonderful feeling that anyone could ever have - to be loved unconditionally by someone.

Beth has made me grow as a person, as a friend and as a caregiver. Without her I would not be the person that I am today.

She is a very special young woman who has so much love inside her and her foundation - The Beth Foundation - is one way that she can contribute to her fellow man as she continues her walk through life.

She is a gift from God, and her life is making a difference in the lives of many children less fortunate than herself.

Thank you, Beth, for your warmth and caring. May you continue to enrich the lives of your family and friends and the children you are helping with your foundation.

With deepest gratitude and love,

Shannon

## The Year Is 2007

In the winter of 2007, daughter Katie, the curly blonde who always made her pride for her sister crystal clear, stood on a stage at the University of Virginia in Charlottesville. She was a beaming high-school senior, ready to head off to Virginia Tech in the fall. She had just landed on the all-state forensics team for her serious dramatic interpretation of an original piece she'd written about the stunning communications breakthrough from her older severely disabled sister.

Katie was familiar with an on-stage presence; she'd starred in her high school's one-act plays and musicals, playing Frenchie in "Grease" and Mrs. Thenaudier in "Les Miserables." And she was a strong advocate for her older sister and for disabilities in general. She was always on hand for Special Olympics events.

When she was little, she engaged her sister in play, trying to force Beth's hands apart to help her pick up her doll - whose name was Hagalegia - and hold and hug it. Beth fought her to keep her hands together. It was a therapist's dream to watch the feisty, bossy little Katie dictate how her sister should interact with her and all of her playthings. Sensory integration was happening at a very early age from a very, very young teacher!

And when Beth won the battle, Katie let her know she should play with her sister, but she'd forgive her for that moment and turn her attention to something else.

The powerful influence of Beth on her younger sister would eventually play out at an Ivy League school in Manhattan, New York.

After excelling in undergraduate school at Virginia Tech with a degree in human development - and experiencing the horrific April 16, 2007, massacre of 32 students and faculty at the Blacksburg-based school only a month before her graduation ceremony - Katie strongly pondered the idea of applying to medical schools. She was zeroing in on the idea of specializing in developmental pediatrics because of the interest she had in her sister's physical and mental challenges. She wanted to impact not just the lives of children with disabilities but also have a substantial positive and direct effect on the parents of those children and the family as a whole.

So she did what any student curious about a particular field did; she shadowed several physicians in the pediatric field to test her level of interest and to see whether there would be enough interaction with families as a whole to fulfill her desire to pursue that profession.

She came up empty, witnessing little time with patient or family to believe she would satisfy her desire to spend enough time with either to make a difference in their lives.

A year went by before she put her graduate school applications in at two prestigious schools - both located in The Big Apple.

Cindy and I were stunned by her choices. Ivy League Columbia University and its Manhattan sister, New York University. And only those two. Nothing in her home state of Virginia, which features top-ranked universities. She wanted to venture into a world of diversity, chaos, color and challenge.

Her new desire? Occupational therapy to work directly and closely with special needs children and their parents to hopefully have a positive impact on their lives. She wanted hands-on opportunities to make a difference. She wanted to mirror the determined and committed advocacy work she'd witnessed from her own parents that resulted in unexpected surprises and communications breakthroughs in her own sister's life.

Breakthroughs like the one that put her on stage at Mr. Jefferson's university in Charlottesville on a cold February afternoon. And this was her performance:

"Sisters"

By Katie Timp

When I was born, I entered this world kicking and screaming, just the way it should be. Make yourself known! And did I ever! With a great big "wahhhh!" Hey, my parents said the doc didn't even have to spank me to open up!

And my hair! Wow! What a head full of hair ... white and wild and wonderful – all over my head. It matched all the hollering I was doing!

But instead of my parents bragging on how robust and healthy I was, the very first thing out of my mom's mouth was, "Look at her feet, honey. Tell me they're okay."

What's the big deal, I thought. My hair was huge, attractive, a real attention-getter! My lungs – well, they were certainly in good working order. I had rosy cheeks and hands that were reaching out to the whole world, saying "Hello, World!" And yet, mom was asking dad about the state of my feet!

"They're perfect, honey," dad said. They're really beautiful." I found out later that neither of my parents had a foot fetish. Instead, there was something else going on, something pretty serious, I would find out later.

Little did I know that I entered this world in sharp contrast to the way my older sister did. She was a mess at birth. Her face was all misshapen and her little feet were folded up to the outside of her legs. One over here and one over there. She was born all broken and bent. This nearly killed the indomitable spirit of my Mom and Dad. They were two strong people but they didn't expect this kind of shock!

The scary thing was – this was only the beginning of some really tough times. You see, once they got the feet worked on, my sister started having seizures – the really awful kind where her hands and feet start trembling and her face gets all distorted. They're called grand mal seizures, but I see nothing "grand" about them. They were frightening to witness – as if someone or some *thing* had overtaken my sister!

On top of all that, Beth didn't start talking when she should have. And because her feet were always in casts the first year of her life, she didn't really walk either. Or stand up, for that matter. In fact, she wasn't doing a whole lot of anything.

Meanwhile, I was a charmer – they called me Katie Lady – and a go-getter, hitting those "developmental" milestones faster than Marion Jones covers a hundred meters! I was walking at nine months, talking at 10 months.

I was the poster child for progress; my sister was the poster child for regress.

What a bittersweet time for my parents, as they watched their two daughters go in opposite directions – and there wasn't a thing they could do to stop it.

***Rett Syndrome is a complex progressive disorder that robs little girls of their independence. They end up needing help with almost everything they attempt.***

***More than 2,500 girls around the world face this devastating disorder. They aren't able to talk or walk, they develop seizures, scoliosis, poor circulation, and breathing difficulties. And they have a need to keep their hands together and constantly ring them.***

*The frustrating thing is they often know everything that's going on around them but they face barriers that limit their ability to process to the outside world exactly what they know.*

*Complex disabilities like Rett syndrome can wreak havoc on the family structure. It can make or break sibling relationships. Jealousy, anger, frustration, indifference and even neglect can occur.*

*Or – it can result in one of the most profound, life-changing experiences a sister can ever imagine.*

I remember how I could play circles around Beth. Oh, she was a great sister because as I got a little older, I could begin taking care of her in my own way. We reversed roles really early in life – me being the big sister and she the little one. I thought she was more doll than sister. She had this sweet smile and her eyes were always shining.

I had to admit, it was tough figuring her out, though. She never really did what I asked her to do.

Beth, do you want to play with my dolly? Her name is Hagalegia! Here, hold her. No, Beth, don't pull on her clothes. Here she is, right here. Don't push her away!

She always pushed things off to her left side. I don't know why. I tried to sit next to her and read with her. "It's your turn, Beth." But not a word was spoken. It finally dawned on me that she just wasn't going to talk, no matter how hard I wanted her to. But she would always try to grab the book and pull it toward her. We played a lot of tug of war that way.

Sometimes I'd catch her just looking at me, as if she was thinking. "Doesn't she get it?" Then she'd smile real big, and I'd give her a kiss on her cheek!

One time, Mom and Dad went off with Beth somewhere for a whole week – to Charlottesville, Virginia. To a hospital of some sort. They said doctors were going to take a good look at Beth to see what she could really do. It was during Easter week, usually a fun time for all of us. But the trip didn't go very well.

Mom and Dad were so sad when they came home. I was scared Beth might be really sick or that she might be dying ... but she wasn't. Instead, they were sad because she failed all the tests she took at the hospital, and the doctors didn't think she knew anything and would never amount to anything. I remember them mentioning that Beth had an IQ of only 25. "Profoundly retarded" were the words they used.

What did that mean for Beth and me? You mean she didn't even know who I was? All this time we've spent together, and she can't even recognize me? Is that what they're saying? Mom? Dad? Mom, what's going on here?

Listen, Beth is my big sister – my only sister! What do you mean she doesn't know anything? Of course, she does. She's gonna have to help me as we grow up. What about helping me with my homework? Hey, I'm gonna have questions about guys, about dating, about sex, about growing up and my feelings and hormones and ...

God, this isn't fair! It's not fair for her; it's not fair for me! God, where are **You** in all this? Is this some cruel joke?

Here, you can have a sister but she won't know anything. She can't do anything. I'm going to make sure she can't talk?

Why can't Beth talk? Oh, but that's not enough, is it? You have to make sure she can't walk either, even though she's trying hard. And then her spine has to be crooked, and she has to have those damned seizures, too?

Beth, Beth, talk to me!  Stop doing that with your hands!  Stop pulling at your clothes!  Stop hitting yourself! Stop it! Stop it!

I'm, I'm sorry, Beth.  I'm really sorry. But you see, all this time we've spent together, and they're saying you don't even recognize me?

I knew that just wasn't true.  Because I know that when she looked into my face, that when she stared into my eyes, she knew who I was.  And more than that, I know she knew that I loved her.  And she *always* returned that look of love.

I also knew that my sister knew a whole lot more than anyone ever gave her credit for.  It was those eyes that told me so.  And it was only a matter of time until I was proven right!

It happened one spring day at school when Beth got a visit from a communications expert.  This lady separated Beth's hands and wanted her to point to colors on a table in front of her.  She told Beth she would support her hand and if Beth started bringing her hand forward to point to a color, then she'd release Beth's hand and allow her to point to the color she chose.  Well, Beth pointed to red and then green and yellow and blue – all correctly!

So the lady put a letter board in front of Beth with letters of the alphabet on it and asked Beth if she could spell her name.  I don't think my mom and dad believed she had a snowball's chance of spelling anything.

But then it happened!  Beth's hand moved quickly to the letter board as she spelled out:  B – and then E – T – and H. Then she continued with I – and then A – M- and she closed it out with S – M – A – R – T!

Mom and Dad were speechless! Could it really be true? This was gloriously profound! Beth had a meaningful form of communication for the first time in her life!

The rest of that day and in the weeks and months that followed, she communicated her thoughts and feelings about life. At one point, she told us all: "Don't worry about past – future."

As for my own unique gift from my sweet sister, well, I received it later that night. When I asked Beth if she had anything she wanted to say to me, she responded by spelling out the words: "Finally, Katie really has a sister!"

The Timp family celebrates Katie's Columbia University graduation in 2010.

The Year Is 2009

My last road race wasn't my fastest race; in fact, it was at a 9 minute per mile pace, the equivalent of my first marathon, the 3:56 I clocked at the Shamrock Marathon in Virginia Beach back in 1980 when I started running the first of my 40,000 miles in life! But as I look back at this race now, the New York City Half-Marathon, on August 19, 2009, I can clearly define it as the most special race I ever ran.

The invitation to run this 13.1 mile race came from daughter Katie in March of that year. She was a couple months away from graduating with her master's degree in occupational therapy from Columbia University, and lived on W. 85th St. in midtown Manhattan in a nice two bedroom apartment about 50 yards from Central Park, her daily training ground.

It had been a number of years, in fact, probably a decade, that I had run more than 10 miles in a single training run, let alone a road race. With an extraordinarily busy life of work and family activities on my plate, including my new role as executive director of our non-profit disabilities foundation, The Beth Foundation, I raced little anymore but continued to run at a much more leisurely pace to stay healthy and moderately fit.

I warned Katie of how challenging a half marathon can be, especially to someone who had not been training too long and had not run many road races up to that time. I also reminded her that August is not the best time temperature-wise to run a race of that distance.

"I'm doing it, dad. Do you want me to register you for this race?"

I heard the determination in her voice, then shared with her a few training tips that could get her to the finish line. I checked out the course route online; it included 7 miles in

Central Park, followed by a long straight stretch down Seventh Avenue that would take runners through Times Square and all the way to the Hudson River. The final 3 miles would be along West Side Highway to lower Manhattan, with the finish at Battery Park.

Throughout the spring and summer, Katie kept me in the loop on her training progress. She'd call me when she had really good news to share about a run. I received steady text messages from her, and could detect some highs and lows in her level of confidence. I strongly encouraged her to get those 10 and 12 mile runs in in July and early August. These would allow her to peak and give her the proper mindset to conquer this challenging distance.

Meanwhile, I was trying to get my 52-year-old legs moving fast enough and far enough to build my own confidence in accomplishing this feat. I had the joy of recounting my training days with Teresa Ornduff and Phillip Prince as I rolled along the dirt padded Virginia Creeper Trail in Abingdon to protect my joints from breaking down.

August 19 was right upon us, and I flew to the Big Apple two days before the race to soak up the city with Katie and build on our excitement for that Sunday morning race. We shared time in Central Park, ate lunch at Mickey Mantle's Restaurant and Sports Bar along the park, and met some of Katie's closest Columbia friends.

We crashed early Saturday night because the race had an early start, and we had to work our way on foot across Central Park to the registration and starting line. Katie and I were assigned to different groups of 1,000 runners, so we hugged each other, wished each other the best and parted ways.

"I'll be looking for you at the finish, hon," I said.

I had decided not to run with music in my ears. Take in the sights and sounds of New York City, I thought. It may be the only time you'll ever run here. And off we went, the yips and yells of runners creating that adrenaline rush that was ever present at the start of any race I ever ran.

The temperature that early morning was a bit uncomfortable, and I worked up a pretty good sweat during even the first 5K. But Central Park was Central Park, and my daughter and I were racing where America's best runners race. It was exhilarating! Alberto Salazar and Grete Waitz and Bill Rodgers raced here decades ago! So I kept a steady, comfortable pace, hydrated at every water stop, and headed onto Seventh Avenue in the shadows of New York City's tallest buildings.

My pace fell off at miles 8 and 9 because the humidity and heat were rising, but running through Times Square serenaded by a Broadway singer and a huge karaoke crowd singing "Footloose" helped push me onward. Meanwhile, I was thinking "Katie" every step of the way.

At mile 10, we took a left at the Hudson River at West Side Highway, a four-lane blocked off for the race and lined with crowds of vocal supporters. Diagnosed as a diabetic through my dad's genes at age 50, I felt my blood sugar dropping just beyond the 11 mile mark. I stopped at a support tent to ask if they had any sugar drink that could help elevate my blood sugar, but they had nothing, so I pushed on to the finish line. The temperature climbed into the mid-80s, but we found out later that with the humidity, it would be New York's hottest day of the summer!

My 2 hour finishing time wasn't a proud moment for me. In truth, my best full marathons weren't much longer. But that clearly wasn't my reason for racing the New York City Half-Marathon. That reason was still somewhere out on the course, suffering through the heat, humidity and fatigue.

I grabbed a bottle of water after having my finishing medal placed around my neck, then headed back to the finish line to cheer Katie home. Thousands of runners fought their way in, some more energized than others. Not unexpected, I became a vocal supporter for dozens of runners pushing themselves down the stretch. I'd call out their numbers and let them know they were true winners at a great race in The Big Apple.

Thirty minutes passed and I continued looking for Katie and her turquoise running singlet. Another fifteen minutes passed and the number of finishers was thinning out. Given the weather condition, doubt now entered my mind that she might have had to give in to the rising heat - until I heard a familiar voice shout to me, "Dad, here I am! I made it!"

A runner's high hit me! 2:48 was her finishing time. We hugged each other, celebrating a victorious father-daughter moment together. Watching her receive her finishing medal was the highlight of the day!

There in Battery Park we shared the highs and lows of our race, then walked to the New York subway to head back to her apartment. Once there, I grabbed a bowl of soup, packed my bag, gave my daughter a winning hug, and headed out of the city back to Virginia.

Life just handed me yet another memorable moment, a breathless moment that added another layer of love to my life!

The Year Is 2010

Beth and I ventured to a faraway land on a pretty Friday morning. Our destination was a school - a missionary school - in the roughest part of the Appalachian Mountains, a place that was universally ridiculed because it was a long ways from anywhere, and the roads leading there were challenging to navigate.

It didn't help that the town's name was Grundy, which rhymes with grungy. This was desolate country, a place where coal was mined to the north, south, east and west, which meant coal dust covered everything.

Other than coal, this town for a long time was only known as a stopover for Union soldiers on their way to the Battle of Saltville during the Civil War. That's until a rather unique school was established here in 1921. And that's where Beth and I were headed on this June morning.

Our destination? A school of 250 beleaguered kids, many of them having been rescued from abuse and neglect. Mountain Mission School took in kids as infants and nurtured them through a rigorous academic setting to turn them into high-achieving graduates. And they wanted to hear Beth's story. I was along to tell it.

This throw-back school tells this story about its founding:

"The time was early spring of 1888. The place was the mountainous terrain of eastern Kentucky. A 10-year-old boy named Sam Hurley, scantily clad, was alone in the woods and was about to 'bed down' for the evening. Day after day he had walked from one house to another, searching for work in exchange for food to eat. His father had died earlier, and there was no income in the Hurley household. The few jars of canned food in the pantry had been gone for days.

"Sam found a rock outcropping which he called a cave and kicked the stones around to make a smooth place to lie down. Some half-decayed leaves pulled up around him provided a blanket of warmth to his shivering body. Then he was frightened. The call of the catamount - coming closer and closer - drove him to call to God for help.

"He prayed for God's protection throughout the night. He told God if he would spare him from the catamount, he would build a place for boys and girls like himself so they wouldn't have to sleep in the woods.

"Sam did make it through the night, and through many more. After some very rough beginnings, he became a successful businessman. He never attended school. At the age of 22, he married the love of his life, Jane Looney. Jane taught him how to read and write. Sam was successful, and, of course, never gave his promise to God a second thought - until a boy, much like himself, came into his office in the courthouse in Grundy, Virginia, and asked Mr. Hurley if he would take him to his house and keep him because he didn't have anywhere to go.

"He told the boy he had seven children of his own and had taken in nine others. He simply did not have room for him.

"Later that same day, when Sam went out of the courthouse to lunch, he noticed that the little boy was sitting up against the courthouse crying. Then he remembered his promise. He immediately visited his lawyer, who completed the necessary paperwork for starting Grundy Academy, which later became Mountain Industrial Institute, which is now Mountain Mission School.

"Sam Hurley brought Dr. and Mrs. Josephus Hopwood out of retirement at Milligan College. Josephus Hopwood became Grundy Academy's first president. He set up the educational system of the school. After Dr. Hopwood's health declined, Sam Hurley became president, and he and Mrs. Hurley moved to the campus, putting everything they owned into Mountain Mission School."

Some 20,000 kids have come through the doors to be cared for and challenged to improve their lives since the school was established in 1921.

Their stories are awakening: "The call came from a man who had lost his sight so severely that it prevented him from pursuing his skilled profession. He had several children. The youngest were twin boys. Doctors advised the mother to abort these children because they believed she would not survive childbirth. She refused on the grounds that children are a gift from God. So, she carried the children to term. While delivering the babies, the mother went into cardiac arrest and the physicians performed open heart surgery on her. This double trauma broke her health and she and her devoted but now blinded husband needed help. The children came to Mountain Mission School."

And there's this one: "A mother wrote and told of her plight, 'I have terminal cancer. Radiation and chemotherapy have not helped me. There is no longer any hope. The children's father died earlier. I want my children to be loved, disciplined, and educated by the wonderful people at Mountain Mission School. I have heard so many great things about you. Please take my children so I may die peacefully.' The mother and a family member brought the children to us. The mother was deeply relieved that we had accepted the children. The mother and her children said their final goodbyes in the MMS administration-building lobby. A few months later, she passed away. This brave woman would be extremely proud of her children today."

And there is this one as well: "Another intact family in New York was traveling to work when a freak storm came up and blew a tree into their moving automobile. The father was killed instantly and the mother was critically injured. She is now a paraplegic. This courageous mother contacted us regarding her situation and we admitted her children. 'People want me to let the social services place my children, or give them to relatives, but that just isn't an option. I want to be able to keep in contact with my children and to know for certain that they are being cared for properly. I know they will be loved at Mountain Mission School. I know they will learn more about Jesus Christ...and I know their needs will be met. Please take them.' "

---

On this June morning, 14 of those 20,000 kids were receiving their high school diplomas. They were preparing to graduate from a school that had nurtured them when they were fragile and ready to give in to life's adversities. They had to be saved from the bowels of horror.

They are Meherap Addis, Maty Getachew Bekele, Melat Bekele, Aizohbay Belachew, Kadest Girma, Zekarias Goitom, Cindi Hailu and Teffera Indashaw all hailed from Ethiopia. Then there was Karen Martins-Lamptey, Selamawit Mengesha, Gelila Meffin and Toleshi Teressa. I don't know their origin. And finally, there was Emily Stiltner and Danny Wilson. I think they were local mountain kids.

My message to them focused on the words adversity and success, words that don't always mesh well together.

"But in my life - and I believe in the lives of you 14 graduates here today - adversity and success are locked tightly together. When adversity arrives in your life, you follow it up with large doses of success."

I saluted the principal and the staff for driving them forward - for years.

And then I introduced my daughter, on stage with me, and shared "In All Her Silence" with them. I opened up with how spectacularly decorated my daughter is. Spotlight on Students award winner. High school graduate. Inducted into the National Honor Society. Voted most respected in her senior class. Voted best chorus member.

Beth taught her classmates how to value diversity, be a caring community, work hard at accomplishing incredibly difficult tasks, and truly love one another.

So where does adversity come into play?

"Can you talk," I asked senior Toleshi Teressa sitting on the front row in her graduation gown. Beth can't. "Can you walk, run, skip, hop, Cindy Hailu? Beth can't."

And so the story unfolded, with Beth there on stage before their very eyes. A story of unimaginable lows and miracle highs. Spectacular and severe.

---

The Mountain Mission School graduates were locked in on this story:

You see, we'd been swinging the world around by the tail! Cindy and I were high school sweethearts from Wise, Virginia - not too far from Grundy actually.

I graduated from Washington & Lee University with a degree in journalism. I was going to be a Woodward and Bernstein kind of reporter and change the world!

My wife graduated as a Hokie from Virginia Tech and was headed in the direction of social work. Before we even graduated, I had asked for her hand in marriage. Fortunately, she said yes!

And so we started our lives out together in Tidewater Virginia - each of making a whopping $10,000 a year - and feeling like nothing could harm us.

We felt like we were in control of everything good that was happening to us! In 1982 - three years into our marriage - we decided to start our family!

We were both thinking BIG family - because we both came from BIG families. Cindy grew up with five brothers - I grew up with five sisters! And it was a given that our family would be healthy!

But reality struck and it struck very hard - and over the course of the past 28 years of life with my sweet and vulnerable daughter, I have learned that I am not in control of all of the individual events in my life. The bigger lesson I learned, however, is that I am in direct control of the success or failure of my life based on how I approach every adverse situation and circumstance that comes at me.

Ultimately, it is our perspective on life that allows us to stand tall or crumble under the weightiness of the lives that we lead.

Let me give you an example. There was a young boy getting off the bus at Mt. Mission School one morning. He misstepped and fell forward, hitting his head on the ground and cutting his forehead open. Later on in the classroom, he was goofing off and happened to bump heads with a classmate. In doing so, he split his lip open and chipped a tooth. And even later, on the playground, this young boy was chasing some girls when he tripped and fell on his arm, breaking it.

Obviously he had to pay a visit to Ms. Cindy Rodda's presidential office. And as she and others attended to him, Ms. Rodda noticed that this young boy was clutching something firmly in his hand. She asked him what he held so tightly. To which he opened up his hand to reveal a quarter. Ms. Rodda questioned him about where he got that quarter. And the youngster said with great delight: I found it on the playground, Ms. Rodda. It's the only quarter I've ever had! This has to be my lucky day!"

Proper perspective allows us to fight back against all the adversity that you and I and Beth face in life.

Well, little did we realize - even after we saw how afflicted Beth's little feet were - that our journey would become as dark as night, that we would come so close to losing all hope for a positive, rewarding and faith-filled life. That's how challenging our journey started out.

And it didn't get easier. When Beth was 3 months old, she began having seizures - grand mal seizures, which are frightening to witness and frustrating to control. She's had thousands of these horrific episodes. They rob her of her quality of life. They scare us to death. But somehow, we have learned to get to the next day.

When Beth was six months old, our world began spiraling downward even more. Adversity was pounding us. We were fighting hard not to lose a grip on life.

That's when Beth's head growth began falling off the growth chart. And a small head can mean a small brain, which can mean developmental delays and possible mental challenges.

That's when I began having some pretty serious talks with the man upstairs about how much more pain and suffering - how much more adversity - he was going to heap on us.

As a young kid, a little younger than you graduates, I had my share of personal tragedy. Growing up in the Midwest, in a town called Hudson, Wisconsin, I lost my best friend in a bicycle-car accident. It happened to be my 11 year old brother, Luke. He was coming out of the school yard on his bike when he was hit by a drunk driver. My dad, a pediatrician, was on call at the time and was called to the scene of the accident, not knowing that his own son would be fighting for his life. It's a fight Luke lost two days later.

And then only three years after dad brought us to Southwest Virginia - to Wise County in 1969 because he wanted to practice medicine in impoverished Appalachia - my father dropped dead of a heart attack at age 46.

And now my first born daughter is born so broken and bent. And I ask myself the question: Is life only about a series of sorrowful events as we watch our own family members die early, unexpected deaths or watch our own children struggle against enormous odds to accomplish what in life?

Is it worth pushing forward to go on - and for what rewards? Where's the payoff for trying to be strong and stoic and faithful to a God who wasn't bringing much good into my life at that time!

And so things got easier, right? No - not so much.

In fact, they got more and more challenging as the months and years passed by.

In 1991, when Beth was only 9 years old, we almost lost her to a very difficult series of regressions. She stopped walking on her own and stopped eating as well. We had to have a feeding tube placed in her stomach so that we could medicate her for her seizures and feed her.

We prayed hard and wondered what would come of this four week hospital stay. And we had to talk life-and-death issues with our doctors, who clearly didn't expect Beth to rise up and move forward in life.

But guess what? God's grace intervened - and our angel overcame this near-death experience to gain strength and survive.

On her 14th birthday, we finally got a name for all that had afflicted Beth. The name of her disorder is Rett Syndrome, a neuromuscular disorder that has affected thousands of girls around the world. It robs them of their ability to talk and walk.

They develop seizures and scoliosis, a severe curvature of the spine that impacts their ability to walk. Their hands come together, rendering them mostly dysfunctional. These precious girls have breathing dysfunctions, poor sleep patterns, limited blood circulation in their feet. And they have a life expectancy that is much shorter than yours or mine.

That - my friends - is a lot of adversity for Beth and her parents to tackle without giving in. There were many times when Cindy and I sunk into the corner of a room in our home in Hampton, Virginia, and cried together, not really understanding how much more pain we could endure. Would life just continue to fall apart for us?

There were times when Cindy's pain was so intense that I would get to the phone late at night and reach out to her loving, supportive parents who lived in Wise, Virginia - nine hours away in the mountains where we are today. I would tell them that I'd run out of hope and that I wasn't sure we could go on. Nine hours later - without asking questions - they were at our front door, throwing their arms around us and offering words that gave us new life.

Like all of you graduates - we dug deep inside ourselves to discover what you're learning about your own selves. That anything is possible. That love truly exists on a wide scale in our world. And that people everywhere are filled with goodness and want to be stewards of God's will.

You found a school right here in Grundy that is filled with that goodness.

And this close loving family has reached out to you to help you overcome any adversity on your way to achieving greatness!

Our perfect angel - in her 28 years of life - has been wrought with so many imperfections. But in all her silence - in all her many imperfections - Elizabeth Nicole Timp has taught us more about the value of human life than anyone else we've known.

She is a young lady who has enabled us to find God's grace in all the broken places!

It is through the daunting obstacles she's faced in life and the multitude of challenges we as her parents have faced in life that I can honestly tell you our lives have been enriched beyond anything we ever imagined.

It is when you face that mountain in front of you that you discover who you really are. That's when you find power and relevance and purpose in life.

The graduates remained focused, the 300 parents, relatives and friends behind them in the auditorium were stone silent as I closed out my story.

I told them of our hell-to-heaven experience in Charlottesville during Easter Week of 1986 and of Beth's success through facilitated communication.

Beth was isolated no more. She had classmates who became role models for her. She exceeded expectations each and every year! I shared the skating party wonders and Megan Hall's friendship with Beth.

Relevant - Powerful - Purpose-filled! We were clearly making strong adjustments to all the adversity that continued attacking our fragile child. And we were replacing it with redefining moments we called success.

As Beth moved onto high school, she continued to be welcomed and embraced by teachers and classmates alike. Point of fact, on her third day of high school in Raleigh, we received a call from a senior who was in one of her classes. This young lady called us that evening and was duly impressed with who Beth was.

In fact, she and four of her best friends wanted to take Beth to the mall that weekend for a shopping spree! What do parents do?

Do we shy away from strangers who want to invite Beth into their lives? Or do we take the risk of allowing her to enhance her life and possibly impact the lives of new friends?

We chose the latter route. We were at the mall that Saturday morning and as we unloaded Beth from our van into her wheelchair, we heard shouts of joy from across the parking lot: "Hey Beth, we're over here!"

And we saw five of the most beautiful high school students come running toward Beth to whisk her away for a two-hour shopping spree.

When they returned, they were talking over the top of each other, so excited about what they'd experienced with Beth and knowing that their own lives had been forever redefined because of their special time with our daughter.

Psalm 30 Verse 11 says to us: "Thou hast turned for me my mourning into dancing."

Beth turned 28 years old just a week ago, I told the crowd. We never expected her to be with us this long in life. But the blessing has been beyond words. I'm dancing; I'm not mourning!

In 1998, we decided to package all of the adversity and all of the success that had been handed to us and roll it into one big give-back.

We established The Beth Foundation that provides financial help to families who have kids with rare or severe disabilities. Our foundation has helped children and their families from all across the country - families and children who face lots of adversity - but who are trying to turn that into success! Just as you have!

Beth has taught us about unconditional love. I know you've felt that here at Mountain Mission School. And she's also taught us about the sanctity of life. That's something I know you know a lot about.

Take the blessings you've been given and stretch them out far and wide to affect others in your lives in a positive, powerful, relevant and purpose-filled way!

Adversity? Success! You 14 graduates know what it takes to stare down the mountain and climb to the top!

Best of luck to each one of you! May God richly bless your lives as you venture from Mountain Mission School and take on the challenges that lie before you!

This has been a special moment in my life. I hope you'll always remember Beth Timp in yours.

The first few to stand were on the front row - the graduates of Mountain Mission School, to whom this message was directed. But the standing ovation for Beth grew quickly, and within seconds, everyone in the auditorium was on their feet, applauding with so much respect and admiration.

My heart swelled at this proud moment, and I stepped from the podium, turned to my daughter, and joined in the long, loud, heartfelt applause for Beth. The moment gained momentum when the crowd clearly saw how much she got it. Her appreciation was expressed in the smile that broke across her face.

Her message? "Thanks, it's been truly great to share my life's journey with you through my dad's words."

As the applause died down, it was time to reward the 14 graduates with their diplomas. Each one proudly approached principal Cindy Rodda and received a congratulatory embrace and that coveted parchment signifying their success. They next shook the hands of each member of the Mountain Mission School Board of Trustees and then headed toward Beth and me.

I extended a hand, then a hug to Meherap, then Maty, then Melat, and Aizohbay, Kadest, Zekarias, Cindi, Teffera, Karen, Selamawit, Gelila, Toleshi, Emily and finally Danny.

Their words of thanks for our story were strong, their eye contact sincere. Best of all, they asked me, almost to a person, if they could address Beth with a hug!

Absolutely, by all means, certainly - she would really appreciate that, I beamed! It was clear they'd listened closely to her story. And they were ready to take that message with them on their life's journey.

Students at Mount Mission School in Grundy, VA, share graduation moments with Beth, whose story drew a standing ovation.

The Year is 2011

Beth and I were out early on the beach at Myrtle in early July, taking a long, slow walk on the soft sand. I had placed her gently in the rented yellow PVC beach buggy, a source of transportation along the water that gave us time together. I had lathered her with sunscreen and had her purple sunglasses on to block the early morning rays.

She was happy; in fact, we had never seen her as delighted to be at the beach. At a younger age, Beth didn't care for the heat or the sun. At age 29, she was now showing a different take on life at the beach. Each day when we got her dressed in her swimsuit, she expressed delight with a big grin and steady hand-slamming down on her legs, a sign that she was excited about what was coming next.

We rolled along the shoreline, gentle waves rolling over my ankles. A few seagulls meandered above us. Few beach bums were present this early on the sand. A few runners passed us. I broke out with a song of inspiration, Josh Groban's "You Raise Me Up," in honor of my daughter. I was in a special state of mind, focusing on this moment of sunrise at the ocean with a person in my life who had created in me a dimension of love and protection that most people never get to experience.

She needed me and I needed her. I was possessed by her inability to physically do much at all and by her ability to create in me a fatherly love that captured my heart each and every day that I lived with her. She was mine and I loved showing her off. I didn't hold back in sharing this special blessing in public settings. Many parents who have children with significant disabilities keep them hidden.

Beth was my star, a teacher of more than the basics in life. She taught depth and breath on how to live strong in the face of daily pain, confusion and frustration. She showed me the virtues of serenity and patience and adaptation to every day living. Little did I know that these elements would become vitally important to me in the months to come. This morning on the beach had me sharing time with a young woman who would elevate my need to be a courageous fighter down the road.

A half mile on our journey along the ocean, we suddenly came upon a huge shell bed. The shells were unique, in that they appeared to be unblemished clamshells, perfect in form and color. This uniqueness let me to the thought that I needed to collect 29 perfect, unblemished shells that would represent the 29 years of my daughter's life.

I told Beth of my plan, and I began to scoop up handfuls of these beautiful shells. It took me only seconds to count out 29 perfect shells and I brought them over to her. Beth was alive and attentive, and looked at these shells with intensity. We're going to put these in a little dish on your nightstand next to your bed, I told her, because they represent the 29 perfect years of life with you.

When we arrived back at our umbrella on the beach, Cindy and her mom were there to greet us. I pulled out the shells from my pocket and excitedly show the ladies my idea. They thought the plan was perfect, that the shells definitely matched the life of our sweet daughter.

The next morning we wrapped up our weeklong visit to Myrtle. Beth and I took one last trip down to the ocean for a last goodbye. We packed things up and headed north to Virginia. Our daughter was in the backseat, quiet as usual for the first three hours of our trip home. Suddenly, Cindy and I heard a very different noise from that backseat, and we turned around to find tears flowing down Beth's cheeks. We weren't sure where these emotions were coming from; we thought she might be uncomfortable and perhaps cramping. Were they physical or from her heart?

I jumped in the back seat to reposition her, but the crying continued. Our daughter almost never cried. It was an emotion we had not seen in the past 10 years. The last tears shed by Beth happened when her cousin, Ashleigh, an anatomy professor and extraordinary friend of Beth's, was heading home one Sunday afternoon. Beth began crying on the couch after Ashleigh said goodbye.

Cindy and I realized that these tears at this moment were all about Beth's sadness in having to leave the beach after a week of euphoria for her. We knew she had a good time; we didn't know it was one of the best experiences of her life.

We comforted her and she eventually calmed down. Little did we know how much this trip truly meant to her until we saw those tears flow from her broken heart. It was a moment that took our breath away in the most heartfelt way possible!

Phil and Beth take a memorable early morning walk along the Atlantic coast line and capture 29 unblemished clam shells that represent Beth's perfect life.

It is late morning on a hot July day. 7-11-11, three days after arriving home from our Myrtle Beach trip. No lucky day for me or this woman by my side. We are driving out of Knoxville, Tennessee, along Interstate 40 in a sea of emotion. Life had just bottomed out for us.

I'd been given my death sentence at a neuromuscular neurologist's office.

"You have probable amyotrophic lateral sclerosis, Mr. Timp. The morbidity rates are this," the neurologist stated as cold and matter-of-fact as anything we've ever heard from a physician.

"Extremity onset ALS. Your diagnosis will affect your legs and arms, anything below your neck. This motor neuron disease takes 90 percent of its victims within five years. Bulbar or from the neck up, that takes 90 percent of its victims within three years.

"This won't be painful; none of this will hurt," he continued. "You'll just grow weaker over time until you lose all muscle strength."

So I'll be paralyzed and then lose my ability to breath?

I froze. I couldn't look at my wife. I couldn't break in front of her. Not that she expected me to be stoic or heroic in the face of this stunning news.

In fact, none of this seemed possible because I was feeling really strong. I was not feeling the muscle twitching or fasciculations this neurologist said he recognized on my nerve conduction test. He began detailing what was happening in my right leg, though I felt none of what he talked about. He brought up the word "denervation" and explained that the muscles and nerves in that leg were not communicating well with each other. He told me my muscles would work on their own from here on out until they ran out of juice and died, leaving that part of my body non-functioning and, yes, paralyzed.

I was 73 inches tall, weighed 180 pounds and had run 40,000 miles in my life, most of them very fast.

And now I was told I would die a slow death from a disease that would dance across my skin along my chest, up and down my arms and legs, across my stomach and back and buttocks. It would eventually work its way to my throat and take my speech and swallowing, if it didn't attack my diaphragm first and take from me my breathing - and my life. It would take a few years, and yes, there were a very few individuals who lived beyond the two to five year lifespan of this motor neuron disease.

Slow progression? Fast progression? Who knew how ALS would attack my central nervous system. This disease was first recognized in 1869 and yet the world's leading neurologists had no clue what caused ALS. Progression? Yes. That was certain, and that was going to require one strong mind, one strong spirit, one strong spouse, one strong family.

It was going to require real purpose and drive in life. Every week I would experience a "new normal" as I adapted to more that I couldn't do and more that Cindy had to pile on her plate. I was being forced to the sidelines. It was all there directly in front of me, and I couldn't reach it.

It was going to require full, all-out participation by family and friends in pushing money to the research specialists who want to find a cause and a cure for motor neuron diseases like ALS, Parkinson's, Alzheimer's and the rest of that ugly family of insidious diseases.

In an instant, my interest in what neurological medical centers like Johns Hopkins, Northwestern, Duke, Mayo, Vanderbilt, the University of Virginia and Emory in Atlanta were doing to come up with a cure so that I could live was alive and on fire.

The neurologist left the room. We'd been handed our second death sentence in life, the first occurring in 1986 with daughter Beth. I stood up, took Cindy's hand and walked over to her parents. I threw my arms around them, looked into their faces, and said, "Let's start living! Can we do that?"

My wife of 32 years was holding it together so well, just as I was, as we began our two-hour trip back home from Knoxville to western Virginia. The diagnosis had us speechless for a number of miles.

"Phil," Cindy finally broke open. "We have had such an important life together. We have worked so hard, we have lived so hard, we have accomplished so much."

And we had. She was a master's degreed special education specialist, understanding behaviors in children with complex disabilities. She was also managing her mother's retail store in a local mall, selling collegiate merchandise, toys, dolls, collectibles and the like. She and I were running The Beth Foundation. As a motivational speaker, I was sharing our successes as special needs parent advocates at disabilities and education conferences around the country. I was president of the local YMCA board of directors, an elder at church, the volunteer leader of a health and wellness movement in our community sponsored by the Robert Wood Johnson Foundation and the Center for Disease Control.

On top of all that, I was helping to run a strong, successful public relations firm in the heart of the Appalachian Mountains, where companies needed strategic communications plans to gain media interest, pump up their brand, showcase their products and services, and grow their bottom line. It was an energizing day-to-day diverse business that was the right blend of stress and success. And I was surrounded by smart strategists, writers and graphic designers.

"We have lived life hard, Cindy," I concurred. "I have no regrets. It has been saturated with beauty and love. And I'm not going to even begin to ask why on this one."

"Phil, I have to tell you that what I am feeling right now is something I have never felt before. We could have been married another 40 years, and if this diagnosis had not come up in our lives, I don't know that I ever would have found or felt the depth of love I have in my heart right now for you."

That rock-of-gibraltar statement took my breath away.

"Phil, I know it's hard to believe this, but I'm realizing right now that we have been living life at no more than 80 percent. We need to take it to 110 percent right now. Can we do that?"

"I'm feeling it, too, Cindy. I am. Let's take it there."

With my life on the line, I reached across the car and grabbed her hand and the emotion poured from my heart into the grip I had in her warm, loving embrace. It was deeper than anything I had ever experienced. That sensation would remain in my heart forever.

Silver linings, in the face of that menacing black storm cloud that hovered over us every day, began exploding in our lives! They captured our attention and led us to a life of brilliance we'd never come close to experiencing before!

I began explaining to people that I wanted to live a lot longer and not just to live, but to live like I now knew how to live, at an extraordinary level that I had never experienced before, with love and emotion emerging each and every day to everyone and anyone I cared for. It was time, more than ever, to share my positive and uplifting perspective on life with others to help them elevate the relevance and purpose in how we should truly live.

Each summer in July, Cindy and her mother, owners of a retail store specializing in toys, dolls, collectible gifts and collegiate items in our local mall, head to market in Atlanta to restock the store. It's quite a five-day adventure, covering floor upon floor of goods.

Three days after my diagnosis of ALS, these two heartbroken women were off to Atlanta to complete this necessary task. They decided to cut their trip to three days because of the tough news we had received.

As they strolled up and down aisle after aisle looking for the right fits for their store, Phyllis came across a basket of pewter seashells that caught her eye, immediately reminding her of the 29 clamshells I had picked up for Beth at Myrtle Beach only a week ago. One of the pewter shells had the words Myrtle Beach on it. Another contained the words Life, Love, Laugh. A third shell Phyllis picked up had the word Serenity on it.

Phyllis grabbed four other shells that contained different phrases. The problem was the shells were not for sale. They were sample shells, and a sign on the basket containing the shells expressed that message. Cindy saw her mother digging into the basket and walked up to her to question her interest in the shelves.

"These remind me of the shells that Phil found for Beth at the beach last week. I've got to get them for him," Phyllis said.

"Mom, those are sample shells," Cindy said. " They won't let you buy them."

"Oh, I'm going to get them. I've got to," Phyllis insisted.

About that time, the woman who owned those items wandered up to ask my wife and her mother what their interest was in the shells. Phyllis said she needed the seven shells she had picked out from the basket to give to her son-in-law who had just been diagnosed with Lou Gehrig's disease.

The woman teared up and told Phyllis and Cindy that her own husband had played football at Western Carolina University for head football coach Bob Waters, who passed away from ALS in 1989 after struggling with the disease for six years.

"You can have any of the shells you want," the woman said.

When Phyllis and Cindy arrived home, I was given those seven special shells. Dear mom shared her story with me. I teared up, not believing both the heartache and the love behind the story.

"You are the son of my heart," Phyllis shared with me. I had never heard anything that stirring. Yes, it took my breath away!

I kept these seven shells with me for a week, and then it dawned on me that I did not need all seven shells. I needed one shell, the one that said "Serenity." The other six shells were going to the people closest to my heart -my wife, my two daughters, my son, and Phyllis and John Prince.

Today all seven of us carry the shells with us. They are the silver lining seashells that keep us closely connected during this most difficult journey. They are daily reminders that we are not going to allow that dark, menacing cloud to overwhelm us - as long as we remain together in love.

Phyllis Prince, Cindy's mother, celebrates her daughter's YWCA tribute to women award in Bristol, TN.

I'm watching her work. I'm watching my wife suffer. I'm watching her shrink time and panic. I'm watching her cry hard. She was a Rett Syndrome mom the second quarter of her life and now she's an ALS wife into the third quarter of her life. Deserving of such?

I'm watching her adjust. I've been shoved to the sidelines to watch this special woman compete all out against the steepest climb she has ever faced.

She is witnessing me walk through the valley of the shadow of death, and I'm watching her climb out of that valley and head up the tallest mountain to plant the flag at its peak - with gale force winds blowing, snow swirling, a heavy frost building up on her face as she drives that stake deeper into that rock! I don't see her backing down; I don't see her giving in. I don't see her descending from that mountaintop!

I'm watching her live, even more than she ever did before - and she did a lot of living before. Now she doesn't hold back, she doesn't pause, she doesn't hesitate, she doesn't question. She doesn't get irritated at my needs. She knows my capabilities are failing. She is constantly checking new devices, new equipment, new opportunities, and new clinical trials in the world of ALS.

Sunday morning arrives and at 6 a.m. she is out of bed to begin preparing the family and all of our many needs for an 8:30 a.m. church service in Bristol. Beth's needs by themselves are numerous; changing her brief, sitting her up, removing her pajamas and rushing her into the shower to clean her. Her hair had to be dried and she had to be dressed. Her morning meds had to be put together and she had to be placed in her wheelchair. Then it was time to meet my requirements - stretch my legs that had not been moved all night, lift me from the bed using the hoyer lift, get me into a shower chair, shower me, dry me, dress me, then move me using the hoyer lift into my wheelchair. Time to brush teeth, apply deodorant, fix a cup of coffee, warm-up a Danish to get me through the morning, get my phone and my voice amplification system, then help prepare my service dog, Nelson, by putting on his service dog vest, his collar and his leash so that he can travel with us. His treat bag is something we can't forget. Then it's time for Cindy to focus on her own needs. She must grab a quick shower, apply makeup and get dressed in a matter of moments. Before rushing out the door, she throws together a peanut butter and banana wrap that she will down on the 20 minute ride to church. On time? Most likely not. But effort is beyond A+, as it is each and every day!

My wife is living. She is acing every need. She is responding to the needs of her aging parents, reaching out to meet the requirements of her needy daughter, handling the emotional concerns of her other two children as they watch their dad weaken, and responding to my needs, which grow deeper every day.

Her plate is filled with daily requirements that have her darting from one project to another - like a determined hummingbird. Then she stops and follows her overwhelming day with quiet moments of sweetness, kindness, compassion.

Why do I deserve all this? Love and life combined to create a new sense of meaning about why we are together on this journey of heartache but even greater halleluiah!

Making adjustments - what is required? I can't write enough. I can't write it all. I can tell you that I'm looking on with more admiration and respect than I ever knew I'd have for anyone or any moment. But the moments are happening so every day, so frequently, so fast, so important.

Cindy Timp creates moments in countless numbers that make me breathless at so many levels!

---

In all my dying, I've been told I saved someone's life! It came from a niece of mine who wasn't able to shake an addiction to hard drugs that threatened to remove her completely and totally from a life with two beautiful, healthy, happy children and a set of parents who have bestowed large doses of love and support her way for more than half her life!

She's 28 now, but she's been a mess since she was 13, partying all out, hanging with undesireables that lived for another drug high. She'd sneak out of her home during the night, forcing her dad, a physician; to have to track her down and rescue her from another wasted experience. As soon as she wandered into the town in which she grew up, she was swallowed up by trailer trash that pulled her back into the addiction.

Her newest baby - sporting the outlaw name Josie but with a cherub face that melts everyone who sees her - had saucer-sized eyes and an advanced curiosity. She studied a newcomer over, and then cracked a grin of acceptance. But Mom steered off course yet again with Josie only four months old and fell into the den of addicts in her old hometown. They preyed on her, knowing her addictive weakness. They knew she wasn't capable of putting love for her children ahead of a pull toward another chemical high.

Oh, she's not mad at her Uncle Phil for telling her story. And there's a big reason she's not. She was dying. Now she's alive!

It's August 4, 2011, and Kristen is checking into a drug rehabilitation center in far western North Carolina. It's a place manned by former addicts who get it. They're fully recovered, they know who and what they are facing when addicts from families that can afford a significant price tag are putting their all into this iffy venture, knowing that their money could be flushed in a matter of days.

For my niece, that flush was going to occur on a Friday, August 19, two weeks after she checked into the facility. She'd been through detox and didn't like herself or her life at the center. Her counselor called her parents to inform them that Kristen just didn't get it and that she was going to leave the center. She wasn't interested in spending any more time at a place that had its act together.

In fact, she had walked out into the parking lot that afternoon to leave, but the unknown of where she would go in the mountains of western North Carolina intimidated her. She returned to the center with a huge chip on her shoulder that she had no real avenue of escape.

The late afternoon meeting was something she just didn't engage in. And then it was time for the counselors to pass out the mail before bidding farewell for the weekend to those in recovery. Kristen was ready to call her parents for a Saturday pickup when she was handed the following letter from me. She opened it in the meeting room and began reading it. When she came across the words "terminal illness," it stopped her in her tracks!

She picked herself up and headed outside. Dusk had arrived and a light rain was falling. Anger was building in Kristen's chest. A terminal illness for my uncle?

Dear Kristen,
Aug. 17, 2011

I hope you are experiencing some amazing things today down in Western North Carolina! I pray that you see the vision of a beautiful and safe life in your future – with two gorgeous children requiring you to lead and guide them to a beautiful and purpose-filled life!

I believe today that you have reached that place of complete responsibility! I am confident that you have found serenity in your heart to push aside the temptations of life that have taken you away from the real beauty of life – your parents, your sisters and brother, your rambunctious little Jonathan and that adorable little brand-new infant baby Josie – whom I love dearly.

I am rooting for you from the top of my lungs, Kristen! I need you to know that facing a terminal illness like Lou

Gehrig's disease is something I could crumble from, turn my back on my family and dissolve into a pile of rubble. I could easily give up my job and my passion for living. I could sink into the corner of a room and cry all day. I could be angry and ugly and unapproachable.

But that's not me and that's not what I am choosing to do. I am standing strong, facing this ugly disease with the love and support and courage of Cindy and Beth and Katie and Joseph and Grandmama and Pops and Steve and Sheila and Marty and Jacque and Bill and Gena and Phillip and Andy and Jeff and Michael and Emily and Brandon and Ashleigh and Jamie and John Ryland and Ryland and Kendra and Stephanie and Jessica and Scott and Andrew and Will and Sophie and Chloe and Parker and Jordyn and Marcus and Gunnar and Josie and Jonathan.

I am keying on the concepts of courage and serenity and hope and love! I am seeing that the silver lining in this dark cloud is growing wider and wider and pretty soon, Kristen, it will take over the dark cloud completely and show us that there is joy and celebration – even in the troubles that life sometimes hands us.

Be strong! Become super-mom ... here's the deal ... you have the chance to accomplish an incredible turn-around in life that few people face. And after you succeed, your pride in what you've done will be off the charts. And everyone will look at you as a super-hero, someone with tremendous will and resolve to beat down anything in life. You can do this and I believe you are on your way to a victorious future!

I love you, Kristen!

Uncle Phil

Kristen's ugly anger escalated! She slammed her hands down onto her legs and blamed God for the death sentence I was handed on July 11. Her life and my life now both on a downhill slide.

She wiped the tears from her eyes and read the letter again. And even a third time. And suddenly - with an awareness that my life was now in countdown with a worst-case-scenario illness while she was choosing to continue on a track of complete failure of her choosing - Kristen experienced a sensory explosion from head to toe. Her heart flipped from hate to heaven. She felt a spiritual awakening, a 180-degree turn in her view of life.

Joy jumped inside her, maybe for the first time ever! She pushed hatred into her rearview mirror. She opened that letter again and reread it twice more. She had a sensory explosion from head to toe.

"I believe today that you have reached that place of complete responsibility!" That sentence in the second paragraph of my letter struck her hard.

She hurried inside the rehab center with a smile on her face, an expression no one had witnessed in the two weeks she's been there. She stunned both counselors and fellow rehab patients, who asked her what was "wrong" with her.

"What's right with me is I'm staying here," Kristen burst open with pride. "I'm not leaving. I'm going to get this right! I'm sticking with it. I believe I can!"

The emotions poured from her when she called her parents to let them know she wasn't leaving Mill Springs.

"I got a letter from Uncle Phil," she told her dad. "I can do this, dad. Uncle Phil is going to fight for his life while I throw mine away? That's not happening any more. I'm going to win this battle because my Uncle Phil has saved my life."

---

A week later, letter number 2 arrived at the rehab center for Kristen. I had to move her for life forward even further! Dear Kristen!

August 22, 2011

Dawn is breaking this morning and it's going to be a beautiful day, a day when you and I continue our challenging journeys! And guess what! We are together in spirit, pulling for each other to stay positive and focused on our goal of living life to the fullest!

Kristen, God is truly standing by for both of us! He listens to our cries for help and He will answer them in His way and in His time. And in this process, we will learn how to be stronger, more loving, more caring people! I have four incredibly wonderful people whom God has surrounded me with each and every day - Cindy, Beth, Katie and Joseph! And you have two beautiful, loving little children whom God has given you to inspire and lead toward great lives! And because your journey has been what it has been - filled with ups and downs, curvy roads, steep mountains and dark valleys, you will rejoice even bigger than ever when you definitively walk away from the old life and accept this new and liberating life that God is leading you toward!

Kristen, on Holy Thursday of 1986, Cindy and I were in Charlottesville with Bethie. Groups of doctors and educators and therapists ran her through test after test; and she "failed" them all because she couldn't separate her hands or speak. And on that Thursday, we were told that our sweet angel daughter of 3 years old was severely mentally deficient with an IQ of 25.

We know now that Beth is intelligent and understands all; however, on that Thursday, we were devastated and it didn't look like there'd be a tomorrow! I didn't sleep that night because I was anguishing about our future. Cindy was in tears and we hurt so badly.

On Good Friday morning, Kristen, I went for a long run on some two-lane road in Charlottesville, praying and crying and begging God to help me find a way to a brighter future. And you know what happened? He picked me up and carried me - the rest of my life! The two sets of footprints in the sand became one! I mean that! He promised me that I could lean on Him for any challenge I faced, and I found peace and comfort.

Your dad told me you have experienced a spiritual reawakening while in Mill Springs! Oh my! That is beautiful! What that means is that God is there to carry you to any new heights you want to go! Don't try to do things on your own! Lean on Him!

The little card I've dropped into this envelope for you is one that my sister, Anne, sent me just the other day to give me strength and courage to tackle my journey by leaning on God. I have said this prayer countless times every day to help me. But it is time NOW to pass it on to you, Kristen. I believe that's why it was given to me from my sister. Hold it close, read it often, believe it, and then live it!

I have been doing that - and I know, Kristen, that I am bound for heaven! And that gives me the courage to live life to the fullest here on earth! You are God's precious child! Allow Him to work through you forever! He will! I love you!

Uncle Phil

We were on a roll. I was learning the impact my letters were having on this young woman who was trying to turn her life around. I wasn't focusing on a terminal illness that was eating away at me; I was concentrating on sharing my spirit and my soul with someone who needed everything I had to offer. She needed me to keep fighting; I needed her to remain on track in her recovery. We were becoming very close friends!

Dear Kristen,

September 5, 2011

I'm sitting here in our den thinking about you and all of the important friends you've made there at Pavilion Place in Mill Springs! I'm behind those friends of yours ALL the WAY!

I'm going to guess they come from far and wide. I'm sure they've shared their troubled journeys with you, and you've shared yours with them. Please let them know that your uncle is terrifically proud of them for committing their future to all things positive and good.

Kristen, I've never gone off course during my life. I've always had things together, married a wonderful woman in Cindy and have raised three inspiring children. But there certainly have been challenges in life way beyond anything I ever expected - or deserved.

I wrote about Bethie in my last letter and how dark life seemed for us until we turned things over into God's capable hands. But I didn't tell you about losing my job and $80,000 in salary just one month after 9/11 occurred in 2001. I was working for Sprint at the time in the area of competitive intelligence. It was a motivating job and I was making good money for my family. We had just moved back to Southwest Virginia from the Raleigh, North Carolina, area and we were doing really well. I was able to work from home and take care of Beth at that time. And even though the telecommunications industry was not doing really well, I was in an area that didn't seem to threaten my job.

However, on October 24, 2001, after Cindy and I had just closed on our brand new house in Bristol, I got a call from my boss. He told me that me and 7,500 other Sprint employees were losing their jobs. It was a shock, to say the least. What was I going to do to support my family, Kristen?

It was time, once again, to lean on God and to rely on Him to give me the strength to keep my spirits up and look for new opportunities. Kristen, I could have given up. It's scary to lose your job when you're the only one it impacts. But when you have a wife and three children, one of whom was close to going off to college, which is devastating. But Cindy and I decided we were not going to give up on each other or our kids.

I took a job for a lot less pay and I began to work my way back up. Today, I am the senior vice president of a growing public relations firm. We are succeeding way beyond what our founder ever believed we would. I go to work every day believing we will have another successful day at The Corporate Image. I make sure I touch base with every employee and tell them I believe in their abilities. I try to inject positive energy into our efforts! It's a great place to work and we have a bright future!

And now I am facing ALS, which will slowly rob me of my muscle strength and leave me pretty weak and dependent on Cindy to care for me.

It's hard for me, Kristen, to believe this is happening to me because I thought I was taking care of myself and was going to live a long and healthy life. But we can NEVER be guaranteed our tomorrows!

And so we have to have the right attitude and the right belief that our journey is going to end up in God's hands! We are all hoping and praying for a cure for ALS. But if it doesn't come in time for me, I will be ready to enter eternity with a smile on my face, knowing that I have lived life to the fullest.

I want you to do the same, Kristen! You are half my age and have all of life ahead of you! And I want you to encourage all of your friends there at Pavilion Place to do that also! I'm cheering for them! I'm cheering for you! And so is your Heavenly Father!

My prayers continue for full and complete healing for you and all of those at Mill Springs! I love you dearly!

Uncle Phil

--------------------

After the third letter arrived at Mill Springs, I got an invitation from Kristen through her dad to visit her on the 10th anniversary of the 9/11 attacks on the World Trade Center and the Pentagon.

I headed to western North Carolina with her mom and dad and her two little children. Jonathan was 5 and Josie had just turned six months old. I was feeling strong physically; I was overjoyed emotionally through this invitation.

The winding roads led to a place of serenity, where I discovered a niece I never knew. Kristen was calm and secure in who she had become. She was confident in her belief of the 12 Guiding Principles of Recovery; she shared each of them with me and explained their direct impact on her new life.

I experienced three of the most significant hours of my life. Together, Kristen and I walked behind the center down a sidewalk to a place of extraordinary peace. The sun was shining, the temperature was perfect; and why shouldn't it be.

The meditation tree at the bottom of the hill was gigantic; beneath it was a circular deck. We walked to the edge of the deck, where Kristen pointed out a labyrinth where patients take meditative walks in front of a sparkling waterfall. This was the place to turn a troubled life around.

Kristen was new and bright and beautiful! She was a resurrected child of God. Ahead of her was way more recovery. After her remaining few weeks at Pavilion, she would be required to spend three months at a sober living house in Asheville, North Carolina. While there, she would develop a step-by-step recovery plan to guide her future. Would it include college or a job? She wasn't sure. She knew it would involve a continuous round of recovery meetings that would hopefully keep her on track.

There was no guarantee for success. She knew relapse could easily be a choice in her future. But this 27-year-old mother of two also knew she had a level of self-confidence, support and spiritual guidance she had never experienced before. She was soaring!

She was fully prepared to take on any temptation and turn it back. She was taking my breath away!

————————————

A few days back home I was euphoric about what had happened in my life in the face of a terminal illness. I truly felt like I'd taken this horrific disease to a whole different level. I was willing to take on this ugly demoralizing illness if I could save a life. No, I never anticipated that a single letter would make much of a difference at all. Through that letter, I wanted

Kristen to know that I cared about her. I wanted to engage her in fighting for a better, stronger life. I wanted to her to save the lives of her two children. But change her life to this extent?

The momentum was building; I had to keep it going.

Dear Kristen,

September 14, 2011

Where do I begin? All week long, I've been shouting to the world your transformational resurrection from a dark past to a glorious new day, Kristen!

Since our visit on Sunday, I have not stopped thinking about what a beautiful new woman you are! I couldn't believe my eyes or my ears - or my heart! That was Kristen, new Kristen, loving Kristen, caring Kristen, smart Kristen, insightful Kristen, reformed Kristen, resurrected Kristen!

I saw a woman who has already taken her past and flushed it, fully and completely, so that she is prepared to stand strong and resistant against any temptation threatening to pull her down.

In fact, Kristen, I was so overwhelmed by our visit that I texted your dad before I went to bed Sunday night and said the following: "Steve, you should rest easy tonight. You have a resurrected daughter!"

This week, I have taken every opportunity to share my Sunday experience with as many people as possible because I just couldn't keep you to myself! I have shared my joy with Cindy, Beth, Joseph, Katie, Uncle Bill, Grandmama, Pops and a whole bunch of my co-workers at The Corporate Image! They are rejoicing for you!

I told this story to the pastor of my church, Central Presbyterian! He was so encouraged that God is working through us to help you in your complete and total recovery! I told this joyous, hopeful story to a church friend named Nelson and to a business friend name Tom. I called your dad last night and told him I could not stop thinking about you because I was so encouraged about the person you are today - in the here and now!

You are a beautiful, confident, self-assured woman whom I honestly believe will impact the lives of many people the rest of your life! When you have overcome the deep, dark fire pit that you've lived the past 14 years, Kristen, you have a story few others can even begin to imagine overcoming! But you've done it!

I see you as a forward-thinking, positive, proactive woman who will rejoice in living every day to its fullest. Jonathan will be ready for a mom who will give him your very best each and every day! Josie will be holding onto a mom who will celebrate every beautiful, touching, memorable moment with her precious baby girl!

I was driving home this evening, Kristen, and I pulled out a CD from my glove compartment. And the last song on this CD was from the Broadway show, "Wicked." It's called "Defying Gravity"! I shoved the CD into the player and pushed the forward buttons until I arrived at song # 17 - Defying Gravity. There was something that pushed me to do this.

I cranked up the volume because I love this song and needed to hear it! And then I immediately dedicated it to my sweet, newly resurrected niece named Kristen Prince. And I cried as I sang these words:

Something has changed within me
Something is not the same
I'm through with playing by the rules

Of someone else's game.
Too late for second-guessing
Too late to go back to sleep
It's time to trust my instincts
Close my eyes - and leap!

It's time to try
Defying gravity
I think I'll try
Defying gravity
And you can't pull me down!

I'm through accepting limits
"cause someone says they're so,
Some things I cannot change
But till I try, I'll never know!
Too long I've been afraid of
Losing love I guess I've lost.
Well, if that's love
It comes at much too high a cost!

I'd sooner buy
Defying gravity
Kiss me goodbye
I'm defying gravity
And you can't pull me down!

No one can pull you down, Kristen. No one will! Ever! Never! Gravity is that awful place you've been! You've soared far above it now! I know you have! You are God's precious child who is ready to learn, grow and understand your beautiful purpose in this world.

I am here, now and forever, to be your friend. To encourage you. To stand not behind or in front of you - but beside you - all the way to victory!

I love you and confirm my commitment to your new, resurrected life!

## Uncle Phil

Flush the drug addiction. Kristen arrived back in town the week before Christmas of 2011! She is back with her Jonathan and her Josie! She has rented a home. She is focused - not flighty. She is strong but will always struggle because that's what addiction stands for. She is experiencing the brightness of a positive day every day, something most of us take for granted because our lives haven't been shrouded in devil darkness like hers for 14 years. She says she sees things every day that are routine to everyone else but brand new and bright and beautiful and different to her. These new discoveries create excitement in her and are strong signals that she will succeed in her life.

Almost daily she attends recovery meetings that continue leading her in the best direction possible. Her steps forward are careful and measured. In her previous life, her primary focus was the need for a male friend who shared similar weaknesses; now her focus centers on caring for herself first and foremost. She knows that distractions can easily pull her off course.

"My uncle Phil has saved my life."

I gave Kristen Prince a new breath of life! I'll take on bad to make something else very, very good. It's a statement I'll take with me to eternity!

Phil and his niece, Kristen, created an extraordinary life-changing friendship involving Kristen's recovery at a drug rehab center shortly after Phil's ALS diagnosis.

### The Year Is 2012

On the evening of Mother's Day 2012, my 22-year-old son and I headed north from Virginia to Fenway Park in Boston to begin a five-day Great Summer Ball Park Tour. Joseph surprised me with a shirt that had the 2012 GSBPT logo on the front and a list of the ballparks and the teams playing at those ballparks on the back of the shirt. This was round two of a father-son bonding trip that took my breath away.

We had taken our first Great Summer Ball Park Tour a year earlier, in the summer of 2011, three days after my ALS diagnosis. Joseph had planned that six-ballpark six-day tour in the spring of 2011, well before I began experiencing issues with my running and long before I got a terminal illness diagnosis.

An exceptional baseball pitcher, Joseph had lived out his dreams of playing baseball at a professional level and came to me with the idea of us jumping in the car and heading out to enjoy America's pastime together. I encouraged him to line up a summer trip.

Within days, he had the journey planned. We would fly to Minneapolis to see the Twins play, visit my hometown of Hudson Wisconsin, and then head down to the Windy City to watch the Cubs play at Wrigley Field. After grabbing some great BBQ at a hole in the wall diner, we would head to the Great American Ballpark in Cincinnati to see the Reds take on the St. Louis Cardinals. We would travel a couple hours after that night game toward Detroit and arrived the next day for a red-hot Sunday afternoon game between the Tigers and the Chicago White Sox. We were surprised and thrilled when Chris Sale, a tall, lean lefty whom Joseph had pitched against from Florida Gulf Coast University in Fort Myers. Florida, came into the game as a relief pitcher in the sixth inning for the White Sox. He was brilliant, striking out five batters in two innings, and would actually become a Cy Young candidate the very next year for the Sox as a starter. Our next stop was at PNC Park in Pittsburgh, and we closed out our Great Summer Ball Park Tour with a visit to Camden Yards in Baltimore, the place where George Herman "Babe" Ruth was born.

Joseph set up our 2012 Great Summer Ball Park Tour as a visit to some of America's biggest cities, including Boston, Philadelphia, New York City and Washington, D.C. Fenway Park was celebrating its 100th anniversary, and on the way to Fenway we picked up my sister Anne and her husband John in Quaker Hill, Connecticut. Rainy, cool weather tried to put a damper on this game but the baseball gods were with us. The rain stopped just before Jon Lester, a cancer survivor and the starting pitcher for the Red Sox, took the mound and spun a 6 to 1 win against the Seattle Mariners. We were treated to front row seats overlooking the bullpen in left field, and the great Green Monster was just off to our right, creating the perfect atmosphere for a couple of baseball lovers like my son and me.

We headed back to Quaker Hill for a very short night of sleep, and then jumped in the car to fast track it to Philadelphia for a 1 o'clock game between the Phillies and the Astros. My son drove through pounding rain for hours, and the weather forecast was more than gloomy, with a prediction of rain at 80% throughout the afternoon. We took pictures, as we did at every stadium, of the great bronze statues surrounding Phillies stadium, and then headed inside. Once again, the baseball gods protected us with surprising sunshine and clear skies the entire afternoon. We planted ourselves in the upper deck looking straight down on home plate, with the City of Brotherly Love in the distance behind the outfield wall. Former tennis great Billie Jean King threw out the first pitch to the Philly fanatic, which set the stage for a great game. This ballgame was an extra inning thriller, as Hunter Pence hit a walk off homer into the left-field bleachers in the 11th inning for a Phillies victory.

Our next stop was in Flushing, New York, a night visit to Citi Field to celebrate the 50th anniversary of the New York Mets organization and to see the Mets play the Reds. We had all day to enjoy a stop in Manhattan, and our choice was to visit the 9/11 Memorial in lower Manhattan. Witnessing the twin memorial pools honoring the names of every person who died in the terrorist attacks on September 11, 2001, and February 26, 1993, was moving and extraordinarily reverent to both of us.

We had some questions and found a tour guide to help us gain a better understanding about the future of the seven-story underground memorial that was still not open to the public. The tour guide, a former investment broker who witnessed the 9/11 attacks from his 30th story office a couple blocks from the World Trade Center, answered our questions, and then asked me why I was in a wheelchair. I told him about my disease, and he immediately mentioned the survivor tree and my need to visit it before we left the 9/11 Memorial.

Obviously, we wanted to know the importance of this tree. The tour guide shared with us that this callery pear tree was originally planted in the vicinity of buildings four and five at the World Trade Center complex in the 1970s. It was supposed to live no more than 20 years, but this tree lived 30 years but was only 8 feet tall when it was crushed under five stories of concrete during the 9/11 attacks. Most of the tree was destroyed when the towers fell. With lifeless limbs, snapped roots and a blackened trunk, it had little chance of survival. However, it was plucked from the wreckage and was nursed back to health at the Arthur Ross Nursery at Van Cortlandt Nursery in the Bronx.

According to the tour guide, this small tree began to flourish for the next 10 years until it was uprooted by a storm. On December 22, 2011, the tree was replanted at the 9/11 Memorial. It now stands 35 feet tall - and I got my hands all over it during our visit!

I witnessed cuts and bruises and scars all over this tree. We were told visitors came from all over the world to touch this tree in the hope that there illness might receive a miracle turnaround. I can't deny that I suddenly had the same hope and dream for this incurable disease known as ALS. And I don't doubt that my son experienced that same feeling of hope for his dad.

We left the 9/11 Memorial on a high and headed off to Citi Field to see Mets ace pitcher Johan Santana, the guy who had tossed a no-hitter in his previous start, throws seven strong innings of one run ball against the Cincinnati Reds. Unfortunately, his bullpen couldn't hold a 3 to 1 lead and the Mets lost 6-3.

Our next stop was Nationals Park in Washington D.C. to see 19-year-old rookie Bryce Harper and the Nationals play back-to-back games against the Pittsburgh Pirates and the Baltimore Orioles. We enjoyed that Battle of the Beltway game between the Nationals and Orioles with my sister, Gemma, and her husband, Bruce, who are big O's fans. The game was a nail biter and ended with drama when Orioles right fielder Joe Markakis slammed an upper deck solo homer to give his team a 2-1 victory.

My baby sister created a moment that took my breath away when, in the bottom of the fifth, the jumbo screen in center field began scrolling up names of individuals honored for special reasons. And up popped our names - Phil and Joseph Timp, representing Team Timp! I snapped a photo, or maybe three, to capture that memory from sister Gemma! And I was more than happy that her favorite team, the O's, won that game in dramatic fashion!

It was the perfect ending to another father-son Great
Summer Ball Park Tour!

Father and son share a "great summer ball park tour" with a
stop at Comerica Park in Detroit in 2011.

When the end-of-life has some degree of predictability,
it's time to consider taking a trip to a place you'd always wanted
to visit but never felt like you could afford it. Since our wedding
in 1979, Cindy had in her heart the desire to visit "paradise,"
a.k.a. the islands of Hawaii, and more specifically Kauai. But
chaos arrived in our lives in 1982, and we put that visit to
Hawaii way far back in the rearview mirror as we took on our
mountain climbing challenges.

One evening in the spring of 2012, a good eight months
into my disease, Cindy sat down at the kitchen table for dinner.
I was sitting on the couch in the den with my laptop computer.
Earlier that afternoon, Hawaii had come to my mind for the

first time in decades, and I had done a little research on that paradise place. I had never, ever done that before, but things happen for a reason. My wife looked up from her dinner plate and shocked me with the question, " I think we need to go to Hawaii, Phil!"

"Are you kidding me?" I responded with a huge smile on my face that surprised Cindy. " I was going to ask you that very same question this evening! I was researching the islands this afternoon! Are you serious? Then let's go!"

Given my declining physical status, which included significant weakness in my right leg and the need to travel in some kind of wheelchair, we didn't know how a trip like this could really happen in an adventureland like Hawaii. Given the determined couple we are and knowing the many mountains we had already climbed, this venture wasn't going to overwhelm us by any stretch of the imagination.

The one thing we needed was someone to accompany us on this journey, someone we could share our fears and our joys with and laugh and cry with as we would obviously ponder in this place called Paradise what fears we would be facing. I needed a confidant to express my concerns to on what was out in front of me and how I should handle it. Cindy needed that very same person, someone who listened intently and then provided gentle words of support that would help us clear hurdle after hurdle. That confidant also needed to be someone who would double us over in laughter when we needed it most.

Cindy picked the phone up and called brother Steve, a dear friend who over the course of our entire marriage had become our family doctor, responding both day and night to quirky aches and pains from every member of our family. He was the kind of guy who never once complained about being overwhelmed by the volume of calls or the nature of those calls. He never ignored our requests for help and always gave us an answer we needed. but he was way more than a family physician for us. We had a strong family connection for deep needs, helping each other in any way possible to work through issues that created stress and threatened to harm our individual families.

My deep and abiding outreach to Kristen that changed her life was just one example of how close our two families became tied together. Living with ALS and its upcoming assault on me would reach stages that more than just my wife and I could handle by ourselves.

Keep in mind, Steve wasn't a loner. it wasn't that he had a lot of free time to spend with us. He had a full medical schedule as a hospitalist in Greeneville, Tennessee. He had a wife, four daughters and a son - and a slew of grandchildren, with more on the way. He was 'old dad', the attraction that kept this family fired up and moving forward in a positive direction, regardless of the often overwhelming challenges it had to face.

Imagine the role he had to play on a daily basis responding to not only the medical needs of wife and children, but what to do when grandbabies named Marcus, Gunnar, Jonathan, Josie, Parker, Jordyn, Carson and Hadleigh developed the routine crud that all babies have to fight through!

"Steve, Phil and I just decided we're going to Hawaii this summer! Will you and Sheila go with us?"

Without hesitation, the answer was a very strong yes. He hadn't asked his wife. He hadn't looked at his hospitalist schedule for the month of June. All he heard was a need from his only sister, and his confirmation was absolute. A man whose plate was overflowing on a daily basis had no issue piling even more on that plate to be there emotionally for his sister and her husband whom he called his brother.

Late June of 2012 wound up being the perfect time to take a 10 day trip to a place where the average daily temperature was 78°. It was a time when most of the United States caught fire, particularly in the South, where temperatures escalated to more than 105°.

Maui was our first stop, and the Road to Hana was a wild, nine-hour, stop-and-go adventure around the entire island in a red convertible Wrangler. Lush was redefined along this trip, as we witnessed breathtaking waterfalls and an unblemished landscape. We clearly understood why this journey was labeled The Land That Time Forgot. It was something this foursome would never forget!

The winding, twisting roads that had our wives screaming in fear at times made our Appalachian roadways back home seem smooth and easy. There were far too many single lane dirt roads that led us into blind curves, requiring Steve to blast his horn ahead of time so that we might avoid a head-on collision. This road often plunged us straight down to the ocean shoreline, leaving us breathless. But it was our time in life to take these chances, throw aside all fear, and let our screams of delight fill the Pacific Ocean air.

The sunsets resting on the water were moments all visitors teed up to highlight their evenings. Crowds gathered on the veranda to experience that "green line" explosive moment when the sun disappeared on that distant ocean horizon. It was a moment that created an excitement that we never knew existed.

Then it was off to St. Regis in Kauai, a western island that was clearly paradise on steroids for the four of us! This five-star resort overlooks Hanalei Bay, the place where Peter Yarrow of Peter, Paul and Mary wrote "Puff, the Magic Dragon" after envisioning a dragon form in the mountains across the bay. Or something like that. Regardless, the place was a dreamland for us. The mountains across the bay, highlighted by brilliant waterfalls, received 400 inches of rain a year, the wettest place in the world. But our week there was one of sunshine and glory, despite the weakened state of my right leg, which limited our exploratory options on this grand island.

We couldn't climb the trails that led to even greater beauty in those lush mountains, but we rented a beach buggy that more than challenged Steve and Cindy to pull me along

iong stretches of sandy beaches to reach areas where snorkeling became our biggest thrill on this memorable trip.

I struggled to get in the water, but my brother-in-law made sure I wasn't going to back down in this snorkeling venture. He tackled me in the water, grabbed my weakened right foot and battled courageously to get that flipper on that foot.

My three companions took on the challenge of ensuring that I would experience not only the beauty of the coral reef and the millions of colorful, fanciful fish in and around Hanalei Bay, but that I would also witness their extraordinary outreach of love to guide me - weak as I was - through the water by holding my hand and moving me in, out and around the coral reef so that I could experience the beauty of the schools of fish that occupied those coves. They recognized my limited energy; a 20-minute snorkeling adventure was about all I could handle. When we arrived back at the shoreline, the emotions expressed by Sheila and Steve, the importance of sharing this last-time experience with me, enabled me to recognize the depth of love this couple had for my wife and me.

We shared long, important conversations in the evenings around the pool under a blue moon, reminiscing about the fun we had as couples sharing time together during our early years of marriage in Tidewater, Virginia. This was an important, lifelong couple to us for a variety of reasons. Steve was in med school back in the early 1980s, while I was a newspaper feature reporter interviewing the likes of an American hostage captured at the US Embassy in Tehran, Iran, in 1979, and talking one-on-one to tennis star Arthur Ashe before he learned that he had AIDS.

Steve and I played tennis together on weekends, and, with wives in tow, would race to the movie theater on a Friday evening to enjoy more time together.

Our wives became best of friends, with Sheila giving birth first to a daughter, Ashleigh, who would eventually attend Yale University and then medical school before suffering a stroke on her 29th birthday only three months after getting her osteopathic medical degree. Sheila was always by our side as we ventured down an entirely different path of chaos and confusion with our firstborn, Beth.

We expressed the extraordinary value that each of our families shared with each other to move individual lives forward in a positive direction. I shared with Steve and Sheila that Kristen's resurrected life was giving me the inspiration to remain strong and focused on living my life in the very best way

I could, to remain a strong role model for their daughter and be a friend for life to her. This experience brought our families even closer together as lifelong friends, committed to helping when help is needed at any level and creating moments of joy and laughter as often as possible, knowing that time mattered more than ever!

That's what this trip to Hawaii meant. Matching Panama Jack hats for Steve and me; laughter at all the hens and their chicks running loose on the island; stunned by the fact that every attendant at St. Regis knew us by our first names; enjoying ham, turkey and cheese sandwiches on our veranda highlighted by frequent visits from a red crested bird we named Prince.

We snorkeled at Tunnels and Ke'e, took a helicopter tour into the lush mountains of Kauai with a chilled out pilot who mumbled descriptives of the landscape we never understood but occasionally picked up on a few words like Jurassic Park and Kevin Costner.

We had our breaths taken away when we flew along the brightly colored Napoli Coast and later took an ocean cruise along that same coastline, dining on prawn skewers and filets and toasting to courage, serenity, hope and love - those virtues we identified as the most important to live for right after I got my diagnosis. We visited the historic Kilauea Lighthouse and scared our wives nearly to death as we raced along the two-lane canyon roads to stunning lookouts, where we witnessed a Grand Canyon vista, the blends of browns, rusts, greens, oranges and blues on the jagged mountains creating yet another thrill for us.

As big as all this was, nothing took my breath away like the surprise from my wife on Sunday evening, July 1, 2012.

Cindy and Sheila had left Steve and me so they could "take care of some business." We didn't question their disappearance. I took a needed rest and then Steve came by to pick me up and we headed down to the pool in the early evening to track down our wives and enjoy another sunset moment together. Little did I know what I would experience! As I rolled by the pool, my eyes spotted a big, beautiful heart shaped rose petal form on the grass. "Wow, Steve, someone's going to have a heck of a special evening!"

"You are!" my wife said as she jumped out in front of me, surprising me with a gorgeous ginger lai that she placed around my neck. "We are going to renew our wedding vows, Phil!"

Sheila was armed with multiple cameras and began shooting photos of this highlight moment that was taking my breath from me. Cindy handed me our vows - the ones we had written back in 1979 - and we stepped inside the rose petal heart to experience joys and tears in recounting the beauty of a prestigious marriage we had created for more than three decades!

On a pair of legs that were failing me, I never felt stronger as I expressed my dearest, deepest love to my wife. With a terminal illness trying to stifle my drive to live, my voice was never more confirming as I read my vows to Cindy. My commitment in 2012, through those words, was every bit as affirming as when I spoke those words as a 22-year-old on the altar at St. Anthony's Catholic Church in Norton, Virginia, on August 25 of 1979.

My eyes penetrated hers, allowing her to feel the intensity of the joy I had experienced in living with her over the course of 33 years. Steve was our witness as we stood inside that heart at sunset, holding hands tightly and recommitting the depth of our love to one another. Hugs were huge. Tears were defining every step of the journey we had traveled together. This lovely and loving event surpassed even the very best moments of my life! I was lost in paradise with my loving wife and the two beautiful people sharing this breathtaking moment with us.

With this moment now stamped on my heart, my wife had given me all the courage and strength I would need to truly live life with an unequaled perspective, knowing that my body would be on a downward spiral, the result of an insidious terminal illness. Cindy reconfirmed to me that she was mine "to have and to hold, for better or for worse, for richer, for poorer, in sickness and in health, to love and to cherish; from this day forward until death do us part."

I believed every word she spoke, convinced that yes, it truly was happening! It was how we were living!

Special family members, Steve and Sheila Prince, share a surprise wedding vow renewal ceremony with Phil and Cindy in Kauai in July 2012.

In the fall of 2012, before the leaves in the Appalachian Mountains splashed the landscape with maroon and gold, I was on a tear with my talk. Churches large and small across the region were inviting me to share my life story with their congregations. I could still climb the steps of any altar with assistance, but we had a trunk full of wheelchairs to get Beth and me in and out of the churches we visited.

Regardless of my weakened state, I wasn't going to slow down in the delivery of this powerful message. One Sunday morning, the Timp family headed over to Pound, Virginia, to speak to a congregation of 25 parishioners at a 9:30 service. After shaking the hands of each church member, we loaded are goods into the car and headed 15 miles to the town of Wise for an 11:15 service attended by 40 members. That morning, we walked away with donations of more than $3,000 from fewer than 70 church members from the combined services, given to research to find a cure for ALS and to assist patients struggling with this disease. With that kind of generosity, well, yes, our breath was definitely impacted in a huge way!

The following Sunday we headed back into the mountains to deliver Silver Linings at a small church called St. Mary's Chapel in the coalfield town of Coeburn, Virginia. The morning service was packed with 80 church members, and I was moved by their show of love and support for my health and the stresses facing Cindy. Beth was so alive and attentive at the service, and so many people commented on her beauty and courage. Our donation buckets were once again filled with generosity. Another $2,500!

As Cindy loaded up our trailblazer with our Team Timp items, a gentleman named Bobby Kilgore, who had invited us to the service, showed up to help Cindy lift the wheelchairs into the back of the car. I was in the front seat and heard Bobby's question to Cindy.

"Didn't you have a handicap accessible van at some point?"

"We did," Cindy replied. "But after Beth graduated from high school, we didn't need her big wheelchair any longer, so we sold the van. Little did we know we might be facing that need again!"

Bobby nodded, acknowledging a definite understanding of that need.

We bid farewell to the good folks at St. Mary's Chapel who had created another great spiritual experience for us and headed home.

The very next day, our breath was taken from us when we received a call from Cindy's dad, who informed us that Bobby Kilgore told him he felt moved to purchase a fully accessible conversion van for the Timp family!

Bobby and John Prince had a strong relationship as practicing dentist partners in Wise for a number of years. Bobby's message to John was this: Phil's Silver Linings message touched his heart to such an extent that he needed to help this family with its transportation needs, allowing Phil to take his message anywhere he needed to.

I called Bobby and thanked him for his intense desire to do this for my family, but I insisted that he not do this because it was an extraordinary expense. He told me that he and wife Courtney were excited about doing something that would make a difference in our lives and allow me to spread my story. He was doing it, hands down. All he needed to know was how accessibly equipped the van needed to be.

Two weeks later, Bobby Kilgore bought a 22,000-mile, handicap-accessible, green Ford Econoline van and had it shipped to us. It was equipped with an under-vehicle lift and a lockdown box on the floor of the van to hold my power wheelchair in place. The back seat would become home to both Beth and Nelson on long trips to Charlottesville, Atlanta, Knoxville, Washington, DC, and other destinations as we continued to push awareness of ALS. This new ride was supreme!

We didn't breathe for quite a while when this great green van arrived into our lives. Compassion had reached a brand new height!

---

In the spring of 2012, I was invited to deliver Lou Gehrig's "Farewell to Baseball" speech and sing "God Bless America" during the seventh inning stretch at a Knoxville Smokies baseball game. It was an evening of awareness about ALS, and I even had the chance, with my son by my side, to throw out the first pitch.

During the game, I had the chance to meet a woman from Knoxville who had ALS for 14 years. I was shocked when I heard this. Most victims of ALS live only two to five years. For some unknown reason, this woman's breathing function had leveled off in the 50% range, allowing her to continue breathing at a reasonable level. There was something else unique about her; she had a golden retriever service dog by her side, which triggered an immediate need for me. I could use a service dog for a lot of reasons, especially when this insidious disease continued to work its way through my body to reduce my level of function in many regards.

A few months later, we were directed to an organization in Charlottesville, Virginia, called Service Dogs of Virginia. It is a business that invests approximately $40,000 in the training of each service dog. The dogs, generally Labrador retrievers, are trained to help people with physical disabilities, autism or diabetes. Each dog is trained 2+ years in an intense program led by executive director Peggy Law. Online research prompted me to fill out a nine page application, and I followed it up with a phone call to emphasize the urgency of my application.

Peggy listened intently to the ugly ALS story and then responded with the need to meet my wife and me in Charlottesville as soon as possible. We spent four hours learning quite a bit about animal behavior and training. During that time I was introduced to two Labrador retrievers, the first a black female named Birdie, the other a 65-pound male blonde lab named Nelson.

I had them heel on the left side of my wheelchair, walk an obstacle course with me, avoid food on the floor, retrieve items for me, and even open the door for me. Both were superlative in their work ethic. And at the end of our training,

Peggy asked me - with both dogs sitting in front of my chair looking at me with merciless eyes - which one I would prefer to have as my service dog.

"Peggy, I can't make that decision," I told her as I looked at each dog with great empathy . "They are breaking my heart. I want both dogs! I can't say no to one of them. You are going to have to make that decision for me, Peggy!"

Peggy knew these dogs well; Birdie was two years younger than Nelson and was a bit more frisky, and maybe too unpredictable, than the blonde lab they called "the old soul." Nelson had a square face, which said he was strong. He had a blend of soft browns and tans throughout his body, catching the public's eye wherever he went. He was predictable, consistent, and insisted on working whenever he could.

A month later, in early October, Cindy and I were invited to Charlottesville to train two weeks with Nelson. If all worked out well and he and I connected in a strong way, we would bring him home in mid-October. His first big event with me would be the Walk to Defeat ALS at a big park in Kingsport, Tennessee.

From 9 to 5 each day, Peggy worked us hard, educating us on why dogs will do what we need them to do. Nelson learned what my greatest needs were, and we both aced our final exam, a three-hour trek in the historic district of downtown Charlottesville where kids, birds, dogs and friendly people were potentially major distractions to me and my new service dog.

Nelson, a dog of exceptional behavior who studied my face and listened to my voice so that he would follow any command I gave him, was mine! While in Charlottesville, we had trained him to massage my toes using his snout in a click and treat pattern because I could no longer move those toes.

He began to learn that my phone was an important part of my life and that he could retrieve it anywhere in the house if I couldn't get to it. This service dog was so brilliant that he would search the room we were in to find my phone and if it wasn't in that room, he would hustle down the hallway and head into the bedroom. his first search in the bedroom would be on the bed, and if he didn't locate the phone there, his next search would be on my nightstand. If that's where the phone was and he couldn't reach it from his standing position, he would jump on the bed, grab the phone off the nightstand, then jump off the bed and bring my phone to me in the den!

If we went to the mall, he would jump up and hit the handicap marker with his front legs to open the door for me. if I dropped a section of the newspaper, I would simply say, "Nelson, get it!" and he would scoop it up with his mouth, step up on my wheelchair foot platforms and place that newspaper section directly in my lap!

Over time and with Peggy's help, Nelson learned to get the seatbelt straps behind my wheelchair in the van and bring them to me so that I could lock myself in. I would then order him to "jump on" the backseat of the van next to Beth, his traveling partner.

Nelson also has a gift of painting with his paws on canvas. In the course of an hour and a half, he marked his paws repeatedly on four different pieces of blank canvas as we continued to treat him with premier chicken flavored treats. No dog wants to step in paint, but Nelson was determined to make this a successful venture - as long as he was properly rewarded for the work he did. His artwork is now on gift cards that we sell as a fundraiser for Service Dogs of Virginia whenever I deliver Silver Linings.

Nelson attends every event with me, whether it be at a college convocation, a Sunday morning church service, or a civic group setting. And now I close my every talk with Nelson taking a bow to the audience. They jump to their feet to applaud him! I think he takes their breath away!

Service dog Nelson has a close relationship with Phil!

An army of yellow shirts - Team Timp supporters - arrived in huge numbers on Saturday, October 13, at Warriors Path State Park in Kingsport, Tennessee, to Walk to Defeat ALS. At the helm was daughter Katie, our Team Timp captain and a girl on fire to do whatever she could to help me deal with a two-to-five year prognosis regarding my terminal illness diagnosis.

She had reached out to friends from around the country, encouraging them to come to Northeast Tennessee to spend a few hours walking in her dad's honor and to help raise awareness about Lou Gehrig's disease. Jen, Rob, Erika, Noah and Adam came down from D.C. Lauren flew in from Los Angeles. She knew that Shaun from Boston, a college roommate of mine, was going to surprise me by showing up for the walk.

An even bigger surprise was the arrival of my niece, Jessica Prince-Sanders, and her husband, Scott, from Blacksburg, Virginia. With them was their one-week-old baby girl, Hadleigh. Jessica had a cesarean section to bring her baby into this world only a week earlier and had no reason to show up for this event. Sometimes sincere love trumps pain, and Jessica and Scott showed this in a huge way that special Saturday morning!

Katie's social media messages to all possible team members were frequent and fiery. Now is the time; we must fast-track fundraising to find a cure for a severely underfunded disease that has been in existence since 1869. She emailed Tennessee ALS Association information to hundreds of potential walkers to encourage them to sign up for this important event. And she established her own fundraising goal to help the larger team meet its goal of $25,000.

Katie was well aware of the extent of this underfunded disease through my latest quarterly visit to the Emory ALS Center in Atlanta, where I saw neurologist Dr. Jonathan Glass, a man of extraordinary passion in the fight to find a cure for this disease. Dr. Glass has spent the past 20 years seeing more than 2,000 patients with ALS, and he himself will tell you he hasn't been able to really help any of them turn this disease around.

His latest efforts were as scientifically advanced as any being attempted around the country. The work of Glass and his colleague, Dr. Nicholas Boulis, was a landmark trial to treat patients with ALS using human neural stem cells injected directly into either their lumbar, or lower region, of the spinal cord or the cervical, or upper region, of the cord.

The first phase of the trial, started in January of 2010 and was completed in mid-2012, was the first U.S. clinical trial of stem cell injections in ALS patients. Neuralstem, Inc., a Maryland-based biotech firm, provides the human neural stem cells that have the ability to mature into various types of cells in the nervous system, including the motor neurons that are specifically lost in ALS. However, scientists say the goal of stem cell transplantation is not to generate new motor neurons but to protect the still-functioning motor neurons by nurturing them with new cells, potentially slowing the progression of the disease.

We were most hopeful that with Food and Drug Administration approval of a second phase in 2013, I might be a candidate for the slowing of the progression of my disease.

So our hope was sky-high for some degree of a cure as we arrived at Warrior's Path State Park in Kingsport, Tennessee, on the most beautiful fall day of the year. The late morning temperature was in the low 70s, the breeze kept our spirits upbeat, and the trail we'd be walking was lined with large trees covered in golden leaves - matching our Team Timp gold and green t-shirts!

As the honorary family in 2012, our team of more than 140 walkers gathered at the starting line where I would cut the ribbon to get things rolling. Hands were held as announcements were made. The names of far too many victims of this ugly disease were called out. "In memory of" was a phrase that ripped my heart out. I looked around at my family members, and saw emotions peaking.

Team captain Katie was wiping tears away. It was obvious that the overwhelming nature of this whole experience was attacking her heart to its greatest extent at this moment. This disease that was eating away at her dad was eating away at her heart at a level she had never experienced before. I reached out to hold her hand and let her know my heart was with hers. Her grandmother embraced her. I shouted out that I loved everyone around me. Family and friend love was reaching a new height!

Then I cut the ribbon and off we went to enjoy a 45-minute walk together on a breathtaking fall morning. Along the way, I shared pieces of conversation with every member who wore that green and gold Team Timp shirt! I thanked them for their support and their love.

The beauty of that brilliant fall morning created an even greater importance about what this day represented for our family and the other families in the region who too were facing a deadly disease.

Picture taking with groups big and small - arms wrapped around one another - was essential in capturing this important day as a powerful and meaningful event in my life.

Were we still hopeful for a cure for ALS within my lifetime? We had to be. We couldn't give up. but the honest truth is that dozens of clinical trials have failed, and only a single drug called rilutek has been FDA approved for ALS patients because it supposedly slows the progression of ALS by a very small amount, giving patients about three additional months of life. Was there a cure around the corner that I could benefit from? Most likely not. My chances were slim to none. I could research the work being done by every ALS center in the world and my hope for a cure would not rise to any extent. So I didn't spend my days searching for information on the World Wide Web that would crush my daily living. I had to face that frightening truth that this disease remained far too complex for even the most brilliant neurologists to solve ALS. I was not going to falter or fail in my positive perspective on living each day with courage and strength.

That courage was lifted a bit higher for me and Team Timp at the close of the walk when our team won the equivalent of the top Emmys, Oscars and Tony's - another breathtaking moment! We were awarded the top three most important awards presented by the Tennessee ALS Association - we had the largest number of team members supporting this cause, the individual who raised the most money (I took that prize), and the team that brought in the largest donor amount that year, a total of more than $33,000! I gave Katie a huge hug for achieving that level of success! Our goal as a team was $25,000, and the regional goal set by the ALS Association for this walk was $75,000. In the end, this walk raised $115,000!

This money would help the quality of life of far too many people suffering from this disease in our region. It would also help move the needle a tiny bit in the research efforts to find a cure for ALS.

Our team, and our team captain, Katie Timp, well represented the passion that fires up a family when a loving member is forced to travel an ugly adventure known as a terminal illness. This kind of family - the Timp family - doesn't allow their family member to endure this journey by himself; rather, they jump in the pit and take on some degree of the pain in the hope that their loved one is protected by a circle of love that lessens the hideous and contemptible nature of a disease like ALS.

Team Timp drew more than 140 members to support the fight against ALS in 2012!

Latency. It's a word we had to grow to accept in the life of daughter Beth. Present but not visible, apparent or actualized. Maybe but not for sure. It essentially defined her entire person. Over and over again, we gave Beth commands, requests, and pleas. We wanted to know what was inside that little head; we wanted to give her options, choices. We wanted answers to improve her quality of living.

And so we learned patience, to see if her real response might actually emerge in a few seconds or a bit longer. Or maybe quite a few seconds longer. Minutes? We waited. And we rarely got that obvious visible response. Her little person just wasn't able to react with any confirmation through hands, body language, or voice grunting.

As we headed toward the end of the year 2012, changes in Beth's seizure medication had us encouraged that her affect was improving. She had been on an epileptic medication called Tegretol that seemed to be reversing its positive affect on her; it was actually creating a greater number of seizures in her rather than reducing them. We discovered that during a video

EEG test in February 2011 when we had to pull her off of all of her seizure medication to force her to have a grand mal seizure during a hospital stay. In this process, a new personality emerged. Beth began expressing herself from her hospital bed in a way we had never heard before. She was using her vocal cords to squeal in both pleasure and pain. Her eye contact was incredibly intense for the first time ever. When she looked at the television, she actually truly watched the show that was on. It was obvious the seizure meds had been sedating her, stifling her ability to let us know when she was happy or sad.

But vocalization wasn't the only positive affect we saw by pulling her off Tegretol. We were equally shocked when Beth was able to separate her hands for long periods of time!

When sister Katie entered the room one evening, Beth not only straightened her arms out, she threw them toward her sister as soon as she saw her! There was no doubt Beth was reaching out to her sister to give her a rare and extraordinary hug! Katie couldn't believe what she was witnessing, and neither could we! She threw herself down toward Beth on the hospital bed and accepted the most loving embrace she had ever received in life.

We were all jumping up-and-down excited about what we had just witnessed.

The good news was that our daughter's greater personality was exposed; the bad news was we knew we could not keep her off of some kind of seizure med because she would certainly endure cycles of seizures that would take her life. So we changed medications, bringing on board a new brand called Vimpat. We also brought on board a new neurologist who believed in a change for the better by taking small medication steps for Beth. Like us, she wanted that personality that was exposed at the hospital during that video EEG project to be present in Beth's life. She told us we may not get all of what we witnessed, but she was going to try to give us - and Beth - as much as possible to continue improving her quality of life.

As the months passed, we slowly but surely saw a brighter, happier daughter. With this gradual change, we were hoping for less latency and instead much faster response to requests and commands of Beth.

We didn't want to overwhelm her or create anxiety for her by expecting more than she could handle. But with clearer eyes, greater engagement with her eye contact, and a much more frequent smile as a reaction to what we were asking her, we knew she was experiencing at least a modest version of that breakthrough personality we had witnessed at the hospital months earlier.

The moment that took my breath away happened in early December in her bedroom after Cindy had gotten her in her pajamas and had turned her on her side to go to sleep. I rolled in my wheelchair next to her bed and pulled myself up to stand over Beth to bid her good night.

"God grant us the serenity to accept the things we cannot change, the courage to change the things we can, and the wisdom to know the difference." I whispered that prayer in her ear as I bent down over her. That prayer was on the wall in a small frame just above her bed, and I noticed that she was looking directly at it as I prayed it. We had given her that framed prayer for Christmas the previous year.

I followed up that prayer by telling her to enjoy her time with her fellow angels during her sweet night sleep. I kissed her cheek as I normally did, and then turned my cheek toward her face and asked her to give me a kiss.

I expected nothing in return, but I did leave my cheek in place and asked her again to return the favor. "You've gotta give your dad a kiss, Beth! I need one from you tonight!"

And then it happened! Beth turned her head toward me and passed her lips across my cheek and returned her head to her pillow! I got that kiss!

"Woah, give me another, Bethie" I shouted out. "Cindy, come here. You've gotta witness this!"

Cindy hustled into the room, understanding the urgency that something special had just happened. "I need another kiss, Beth." And not once, not twice, but three times she repeated the brush across my cheek with her lips! Three kisses; something I had never received before from my 30-year-old daughter!

Cindy wanted her own kiss, so I jumped back in my chair and moved out of the way. Mom leaned over her precious daughter and repeated that request to Beth. With her cheek close to Beth's face, our daughter gave her mother that same special kiss, and followed it up with an excited squeal of delight.

Euphoria had once again lit up our lives!

# The Year is 2013

The year 2013 has been saturated with daily messages, notes, cards and emails from family, friends and complete strangers declaring that my Silver Linings story elevated their perspective in living, created the desire to fight any painful battle like horrifying cancer, and produced the desire to climb any mountain because it led them to becoming a stronger, more determined human being with a deeper, more meaningful relationship with a higher power.

One such couple named Mary Jo and Lester Prince, my wife's aunt and uncle from Wise, Virginia, filled my spirit to overflowing with weekly cards containing powerful words of inspiration and love. My wicker basket of hope was full to overflowing with cards like this from family and friends.

These life-altering gifts motivated me to live stronger and longer. There was more work to be done. My professional work career had been stripped from me at age 55. This new career called motivational speaking - something that brings fear to 90% of our population - was my perfect calling because my story had people feeling a change occur inside them right then and there as they heard this hell-to-heaven story. The desire to rise up and applaud confirmed the impact of this message. And Nelson, on my command, delivered the encore with a superlative by dropping down on his front legs to express our appreciation to the audience!

Among countless messages, two clearly took my breath away. My impact on Ashley's and Justin's lives arrived out of the blue and stunned me.

Hello, Mr. Timp,

I heard you speak at Carson-Newman (University) yesterday, and I just had to let you know it changed my life. My grandmother has been dying since I was at least 6. Every few months I always hear "this may be her last Christmas", and I'm now 20 years old and she's still living alone and getting by just fine, even surviving Hurricane Sandy (my family lives in NJ). Everyone doubts her, but she raised 5 children by herself with Crohn's disease and is doing just fine by my standards.

My cousin is barely more than 30 years old, the cancer has spread throughout her entire body and she's had surgeries every couple months. She and her husband are both in the military and are constantly moving around with their 3 children, so she is always getting a new doctor. Her youngest son, who is at most 3 years old, was just diagnosed with autism.

My grandfather has been diagnosed with cancer since I want to say 2008, and last we knew it was spreading to his lungs and spinal cord. He won't go back to the doctor to find out, because he refuses to go through chemo and radiation a third time. He just had surgery on his intestines and hasn't healed enough from that surgery to have a hernia surgery he needs because of the previous surgery. My grandfather has lost 4 of his 6 children, one almost 2 years ago from AIDS.

My dad is a retired cop from NJ and is now disabled, but able to work different jobs, he just can't lift things or stand for long periods of time. My dad's best friend was killed by a drunk driver, burned to death.

My uncle died the same way, the two men had the same name. My ex-fiancée is only 29 years old, and he found out on his birthday that his heart is a ticking time bomb and he could pass on at any minute.

Admittedly, I've struggled with my faith because bad things sure seem to happen to good people, and I couldn't understand how God could do these things to good people and why I could do nothing to help them. Hearing you speak about your daughter alone was incredible. I know personally my parents wouldn't have done anything to help me, except probably put me in a group home.

I know you probably will disagree, but you are the epitome of a hero. You strengthened my faith when I finally started to find it again, and I guess, long story short, I just wanted to say thank you. I also wanted to say I'm going to Carson-Newman for Education and hearing about your daughter being incredibly smart when she was considered mentally handicapped reminded me of why I want to teach. Everyone has a brain, thoughts, and ideas, even if they can't communicate them verbally. It is up to us to find a way to allow them to communicate because everyone is worth listening to, and everyone has the possibility to change the world.

Thank you for coming to speak at Carson-Newman University, and I hope you know while you worked hard to leave a legacy for your daughter, you will most certainly have an incredible legacy yourself.

Thank you again, and I hope you didn't experience too much pain today.

Ashley Murray

And then this message arrived on my Facebook page from a recent college graduate from a nearby town. I had admired this kid as a passionate baseball player in our region.

He was a high school rival pitcher against my son and the two had played together on a summer travel team, pitching in back-to-back games at a 19-and-under World Series competition in Fort Myers, Florida. Justin Malone wound up being the Friday night pitcher for Division I Georgia State in Atlanta.

Mr. Timp,

I wanted to reach out to you and say thank you for who you are and what you have done. It was your story and short video of Silver Linings that made me re-evaluate where my next step in life was going to be. After I finished playing my lifelong love of baseball, I came home to what I thought was going to be a fairytale life. I got engaged to my high school sweetheart of 6 1/2 years on June 18th and purchased my first dog, which soon stole my heart.

Everything was perfect and life seemed to just keep giving and giving. They say once at the top you have only one way to go and that proved to be how my life decided to fall. Out of nowhere one day my former fiancée left me with no real explanation. This was so hard, not only because I loved her with all my heart, but she was my best friend. The only thing I had to come home to was my newfound love, Marlee, my now 4-month-old puppy.

About two weeks had gone by and I was becoming content with it being just Marlee and me. One Sunday afternoon I was cleaning out my garage while Marlee ran around in the yard. I saw a car pass by my house, then it disappeared out of my range of site. I then heard a quick screech of brakes and instantly my heart sank.

I ran out of my garage with a million thoughts running through my head but a terrible gut feeling that the worst had happened. My best friend, my life, and my only way of coping with the cards I had been dealt was now gone. I stood there blaming everyone, questioning God, and trying to figure out what I was doing wrong in life to deserve all of this.

I was lost for the next couple of days. Nothing anyone was saying was helping and company was just irritating to me. I didn't want sympathy, I didn't want another dog, I wanted my life to be back to normal.

This was the worst series of events I had ever encountered, and I had no idea how I was going to cope with them. I was scared what my future was going to be like or even if I had a future. I found myself mindlessly blundering through Facebook when I stumbled upon your page.

I heard your story from your video and it seemed like it was the first thing I had actually heard in weeks. It spoke to my heart and made me realize that life is full of joy, and you never know how many more days you have on this earth. You helped me to move away from my past and start looking toward the future. You are truly an inspiration and your outlook will continue to help people who are in a dark time in their life.

It is in our darkest moments that we must focus to see the light and you helped me to see that. Thank you, Mr. Timp. You are truly a blessing.
Justin


I turned right around and fired a fastball down the heart of the plate at this changed young man!!
Justin,

I just pulled up your note and teared up when I read it, my friend! I've always admired your dedication to the sport of baseball - and your ambition to go all out. I have no doubt that you will climb mountains and then MOVE them in the course of your life, regardless of what comes your way!

We discover, when facing the dark clouds that hover over us, our deepest, truest character. And that's when we get a standing ovation in life. We reach out to help others. We gain blessings in all that we do for others. BECAUSE I am facing a terminal illness, I am living the most important years of my life - right now! I am living 110%, all out, valuing relationships like never before, loving God beyond measure!

Our Team Timp just raised more than $33,000 to Walk to Defeat ALS - the leading fundraising team in both Tennessee and Virginia! If you attend church, I would love to come and deliver Silver Linings and have you introduce me! I'm speaking everywhere I can to impact lives with a positive perspective! I'm praying for strength and understanding for you! Blessings! Phil

Another unexpected impact. I couldn't be more blessed.

---

Over the course of the first 18 months of my disease, I slowly lost the capability of caring for my perfectly imperfect daughter, Beth. I have cried countless times alone as I remember the bond and the beauty that she and I shared as daughter and father. Quality of life was my focus for my fragile and mystical little angel. I now ask her caregiver, whether it be sister Katie, brother Joseph, or cousins Kristen or Stephanie, to bring Beth close to me in her wheelchair so that I can reach out with my functional left arm and stroke her hair, touch your cheek, or grab her little hands and hold onto them as long as she will allow me to. I speak to her gently and lovingly, reminding her that our bond has not broken just because I can no longer do what I did to show her the extent of my love over the course of the past three decades.

When I experienced this physical separation from my daughter, I realized how possessive I had been of her within the family structure. And after several months of crushing adaptations to my inability to care for her like I did since her birth, I began to witness the work, the love, and the compassion that her mother, her sister, and her brother began to pour into Beth's daily care. I allowed my physical separation from my daughter to become a supreme silver lining in my life. I am now who they all were for the past 30 years regarding their relationship with Beth, and they are now who I was during that time.

This unique family dimension is yet another breathtaking experience in my life, one that I never would have imagined happening.

Today Beth is able to do more with her legs and arms that I can do. I watch her move her right leg up to stretch it; I can't move my right leg at all. She raises her arms above her head to stretch them. I can't move my right arm at all. With assistance from one of her many caregivers, Beth stands up and moves those thin little legs across the room with great confidence, a smile covering her face. My pride in her is immeasurable! I can't stand at all on my legs, I can't move them.

She coughs hard and sneezes like a wild boar! She's got a diaphragm that blows mine away! I chuckle, knowing she is in many ways so much stronger than I am today. Rett syndrome, as complex a disorder as we thought we could ever possibly face, was kicking ALS around.

Beth Timp was surpassing her dad in so many capacities.

Yes, there was a time when I picked Beth up and placed her in a three wheeled buggy and ran 10k races with her, beating 90% of the race field! Many would look at me with disgust and discouragement as I passed them by. Beth would squeal from her buggy; I would interpret that squeal as a "nah-nah-nah-nah-nah!"

And just a few weeks ago, I witnessed my son push his sister in that same three-wheeled buggy in a local 5K road race, with $10,000 in proceeds going to our fight against Lou Gehrig's disease. My spirits soared, recognizing yet another silver lining in the face of this biting disease.

---

I want my soul and my spirit to clearly outshine, outscore and overwhelm the suffering I am experiencing in 2013. The fight in 2011 was a breeze. My muscle loss was manageable. I was very tolerant of ALS. A cure was on its way. My right leg strength was going downhill pretty quickly with the muscle fasciculations dancing up and down my leg, but I could balance that loss with a special cane given to me from Cindy's uncle Thurman, who was 95, in a nursing home and close to death after working as a railroad engineer all of his life. He would head to heaven in January of 2012. But he wanted me to make the most of that cane, and I did for the few months that I still had the stability and strength in my left leg to hold me up.

Meanwhile those irritating fasciculations began working their way into my left leg, my upper arms and across my chest and stomach. They never slowed down and my wife and OT daughter began looking for a vibrating pillow that I could lean against in my wheelchair and keep these irritations   from mentally draining me on a daily basis. I knew the path it was taking - the exact course that my right leg experienced. not being able to eventually move my arms or legs - well,  I don't think I have to explain the fright and fear when that happens.

Meanwhile, other ugly disabling issues were eating at me. My ankle began to swell as my right foot rolled over frequently when I stood on it. My muscular calf began getting flaccid as 2012 move forward, and my quadricep muscle also began weakening. I went from ankle brace to a motorized wheelchair as my ability to walk disappeared completely from May to October.

I began noticing fasciculations in the forearm of my right arm, which meant my right hand was going to tighten and my fingers would begin to curl and become nonfunctional. I would lose the ability to type, turn pages in a book or newspaper, or feed myself with that hand. With two legs that I could no longer move and having lost the critical use of my right arm and hand, I had to begin to respect my left arm and the use of my left hand as my one and only remaining appendage that would function at a respectable level for me - at least for a bit longer.

In early 2013, I began to have some real doubt about a cure for ALS in my lifetime. ?had heard that phase 3 clinical drug trials were being discarded by the FDA. First phase safety stem cell injections had proven successful for at least one patient at the Emory ALS Center. a second phase was going to take place some time in 2013 but the injection of hundreds of thousands of stem cells could only occur in a single patient once a month, resulting in a clinical trial that would take well more than a year to complete. What would my health be at that point? Was the Timp family going to become a desperate team and pull a lifetime's worth of savings together and rush to questionable places in Mexico, China or Germany where neurologists claim to have all the answers for this disease but have no real proof of their work.

As my arms and legs began failing me throughout 2012, I was still confident in the results of my breathing function tests. They remained in the low to mid 90s, which was way above normal. I was hoping to hold on to those numbers forever. My diaphragm was the last muscle group affected by this disease. I was a distance runner; I had built a strong set of lungs and an even stronger diaphragm that would take me years into this disease.

And then 2013 arrived and those aggravating muscle fasciculations that had been working on me the better part of 2012 began taking a toll on my diaphragm. In November 2012, I shared with Cindy that I had to fight a little deeper for oxygen when I was talking. We held onto each other, recognizing that the difference between weakened legs and a troubled diaphragm was traumatic. not be able to walk after running 40,000 miles, well, that isn't an easy adjustment for anyone. But the struggle to breathe? And how fast that might plummet? That is not an adjustment anyone can handle.

In December during my visit to the Emory ALS Center, my breathing numbers dropped to the low 80s. We were worried, but that number was still considered a normal breathing number; I just had to keep it there, but unfortunately I had no control over where it was going.

We arrived back at Emory in late March of 2013 and my breathing function number had plummeted to 60! It was taking a linear drop; month by month it was falling by 5%. In late May, the number had fallen to 50.

Cindy and I were staring at face of death in a matter of months, not years. I had been identified as an "outliar" by my neurologist when he first saw me; I was a guy who would live 5 to 7 years with ALS.

This disease, however, was taking its own unexpected path throughout my body - and my diaphragm was clearly its primary fast-track destination.

This ugly pathway was making life, and the days I have left, a time to create events with my beautiful family that gave me the opportunity to peak life at an all-time high!

A trip the Outer Banks off the North Carolina coast was planned for September, but we moved it up to July because of my breathing issues. Family members would grab a few days here and there to make their way to our big beach house to enjoy memorable sunrise and sunset moments with the guy they love dearly.

My son and I had to squeeze in a 2013 Great Summer Ball Park Tour but couldn't travel too far because of my failing health. So on Father's Day, with Cindy as our caregiver by our side, we headed to Turner Field in Atlanta for a three-ballgame visit to see the Braves play the Mets! Knowing this was our final ballpark tour - our extraordinarily special father-son venture - Joseph had worked out a special opportunity for us to be on the field during batting practice before the Monday evening game! As weak as I was, this special trip cranked up my energy level to a whole new height!

With the help of a tour guide named Kevin, we toured Turner Field, visiting a great baseball museum that introduced me to a baseball fact that I never knew - Babe Ruth at one point was a member of the Boston Braves! We eventually worked our way down to the field and were standing no more than 10 feet from all-star ballplayers surrounding a batting cage with names like Heyward, Freeman, Upton, Uggla, and McCann on the back of their uniforms. Kevin told us to be patient, that if ballplayers wanted to visit with fans, they would come to us. It took me a ton of effort to suppress my adrenaline and keep from shouting out to first baseman Freddie Freeman that I needed a hug from him!

The real excitement exploded when, out of nowhere, Braves second baseman Dan Uggla, a brute of a man with massive forearms, walked up to us with a smile on his face and ask us how we were doing! His sincerity was obvious and you wished me - and our family - the very best in fighting ALS. Joseph had picked up a major league baseball in case we had the opportunity to get a player's autograph. Dan was our number one signature, but it didn't stop there.

A five-foot seven-inch utility outfielder with a unique goatee named Reed Johnson was smitten by Nelson and paid us a visit next. He gave us a good 10 minutes of his time. Outfielder Jordan Schafer was our third autograph, and then my wife surprised me by hustling over to get the attention of superstar outfielder Justin Upton. "You have to meet my husband!" she insisted. He was on it, and walked over to shake my hand, a big smile lighting his face. He grabbed Joseph's hand and told us he was supporting our family's battle against this terminal illness. Pitcher Paul Maholm was also generous with his time with us.

Tour guide Kevin couldn't believe what he was witnessing. "Most visitors might get a single autograph! You guys are on fire!"

The field tour wasn't over just yet. I recognized John Schuerholz, the long time Braves general manager, as he walked in front of us. "Mr. Scherholz, how are you?" I didn't hesitate to reach out to a Braves legend. He stopped immediately, shook our hands and I shared with him our journey with Lou Gehrig's disease and my successes as a distance runner. He wished us the very best. As we headed along the first base dugout to close out our on the field visit, Braves pitching coach Roger McDowell stopped to speak to us and get his hands on Nelson! He, too, expressed sincerity in our fight to beat ALS. I had fun telling him that my son was a good enough pitcher to throw a 90 mile an hour fastball; he was impressed - but didn't sign Joseph up with the contract on the spot!

That night, heavy rains hit the Atlanta area and delayed the seven o'clock game until 11 PM! The first pitch was thrown at 11:10 but we stuck with it through the first six innings until my exhaustion required us to head to the hotel. The Mets had taken a 1-0 lead as we headed out of Turner Field. when we arrived at the hotel, we learned that the Braves' first baseman had hit a walk off two run homer to win the game for Atlanta!

That moment obviously closed out a day of perfection for dad and son on our Great Summer Ball Park Tour of 2013!

---

The next 2013 wonderfully breathless moment also happened in June and was created by daughter Katie, who brought a flood of tears when she invited me to a Sunday afternoon trip to Knoxville, Tennessee, to a wedding gown store to let me pick out the wedding dress she would wear when she gets married!

I was anticipating a roller coaster of emotions, expecting to shed tears with each dress Katie tried on, thinking far ahead to the stupendous milestone moment when my daughter said, "I do," to the man of her future. But those tears didn't fall, not a single drop.

Instead, my face was filled with two hours of pure joy; I lived in the moment. I had never smiled for two hours like I did that special Sunday afternoon!

Sharing the moment, of course, were family members John and Phyllis, along with sister-in-law Sheila, my chosen photographer who had done a superlative job in Kauai during our wedding vows renewal ceremony! We got equal brilliance this time around too!

Katie's first dress choice got big thumbs up from her grandfather and me. From top to bottom, it was lacy perfection; others Katie tried on just didn't come close to matching dress number one.

In the end, Katie's choice was our choice! One day, she will dazzle the crowd as she walks down the aisle in all her beauty - and with the memory of this June 2013 Sunday shared with her dad in the forefront of her mind!

Katie shared a special Sunday with her Dad by inviting him to help pick out the wedding gown she will eventually wear at her wedding.

## Looking Toward Eternity

Bittersweet is the primary word that is screaming at me in every aspect of my daily living. Beautiful things arrive each and every day now at the house to lift my spirits; cards via pony express, text messages from family members all over the country, Facebook messages expressing inspiration and motivation based on my positive perspective, phone calls wondering how I am feeling.

"Staying strong in spirit," is my most frequent response. Physically, I am failing fast, but I don't focus on that as an answer to those who love me. I don't want to scare them. My diaphragm is falling apart. The only way my wife can move me now is by way of a hoyer lift, using a sling to pick me up from my bed and carry my 170 pounds to my wheelchair. If my son is around, at 6'3" and

215 pounds, we can avoid the hoyer lift because he is strong enough to pick me up and get me where I need to go. I require therapeutic movement of my legs to avoid blood clots. I need my arms stretched each day so they don't tighten up and become completely immobile. The nasty fasciculations aren't slowing down and have now advanced to my neck and cheeks, creating a chattering affect that frightens me.

We get bittersweet healthcare breaks because I have Lou Gehrig's disease. I file for Social Security disability and immediately get Medicare coverage only because I have ALS; everyone else who files for Social Security disability has to wait two years to get Medicare coverage. I get the best service dog ever within a two-month timeframe because I have ALS; most applicants have to wait two years to get their dog.

March arrives in 2013 and we are off to Atlanta to my quarterly ALS clinical visit at Emory. I am a patient in a biomarkers study that includes a spinal tap that will try to determine how my spinal fluid and blood will compare to the fluids of other patients. My neurologist believes there are way too many versions of ALS that has complicated the reason the cause of this disease has not been discovered yet in the 140+ years that it has been recognized. He believes that a close look at the bodily fluids of dozens and dozens of ALS patient will help determine the similarities and differences between and among those patients. I'm very willing to experience a few needle sticks to potentially help with the future of a cure for ALS.

Meanwhile, at my clinical appointment, my strength test falls off significantly from my December 2012 numbers. But the biggest fear occurs when I blow into the breathing apparatus and my number comes up as a shocking 58! I don't look my wife in the eyes, knowing I will see tears welling up in hers. My number in December 2012 was an 85. This drop-off was at cliff level. Was my diaphragm failing this rapidly? What would the numbers look like at my next appointment in August?

Would I even be breathing then?

It is now mid-May, and I continue to deliver my Silver Linings presentation as often as I can but in varied forms because my breathing has significantly affected my ability to speak clearly. I now open with what Silver Linings stands for - my focus on that brilliant outline of the dark, menacing cloud that has hovered over the length of my 56 years of life, allowing me to live at 110 percent. Then I save oxygen by sharing my recorded story captured on my CD, and close with my studio recorded version of "Amazing Grace, My Chains Are Gone" because I can no longer sing.

I close my sermon with perhaps the most significant and solidifying earth-to-heaven Scripture verses present in the Bible: 2 Corinthians 4:16-18 - "Though outwardly we are wasting away, yet inwardly we are being renewed day by day. For our light and momentary troubles are achieving for us an eternal glory that far outweighs them all. So we fix our eyes not on what is seen, but on what is unseen. For what is seen is temporary, but what is unseen is eternal."

I now have a customized wheelchair that allows my seat to raise up 8 additional inches when I speak, giving me the chance to look eye to eye with the people I have shared by lifetime journey with. It also gives me the opportunity to throw my remaining functional left arm around these very people to give - and get - a much tighter embrace from them!

There will be a time when ALS will want to take my breath from me. I have decided that I will determine that time, that moment. I will then head to a place of paradise, a place known as eternity, a place that leaves this pain and suffering far behind. But I will never be absent from the breathtaking milestone moments that will occur in the lives of my dear family members in the years to come. They will feel me living each of those special moments with them!

Until then, I will continue pushing the daily pain and agony of this wicked, crippling disease aside to enable my life to peak. I will remain surrounded by the beauty of family and loving friendships and will continue sharing my story to those wanting to hear it.

More than anything, I will continue experiencing life-altering events like those that have taken my breath away in this life of amazing grace!

I am grateful to have lived out this special Indian proverb, and encourage you to do the same: "When you were born, you cried and the world rejoiced. Live your life so that when you die, the world cries and you rejoice!

Phil with a celebratory smile on his face!

## *Acknowledgements*

I acknowledge the following individuals and organizations that have supported my positive perspective on living against daunting obstacles throughout my 56 years of life led by my Lord and Savior; Loving family members Cindy, Beth, Katie and Joseph; my service dog Nelson and his buddy Dunkin; daily love and support from John and Phyllis Prince and compassionate care from Marty and Jacque, Emily and Brandon, John and Kate, Chris and Stephanie, Steve and Sheila, Ashleigh and Jamie, Parker, Jordyn, Brayden, Jessica and Scott, Hadleigh, Kristen, Jonathan, Josie, Stephanie, Marcus, Gunnar, Carson, Ryland and Kendra, Bill and Gena, Will and Carrie, Andrew and Norah, Phillip and Andrea, Sophie, Chloe, Jeff and Michael, Mary Jo, Lester and Jill.

I also acknowledge the courage of my mother, Rose Walleze and the loving support of my sisters and their families, including Anne and John Bradley, sons Paul and Ben, daughter Lora, Sarah and Jim Henkel, sons James and Luke, Helen Reed and Frank Bjione, sons Elliott and Harrison, Gemma & Bruce Dehnbostel, AnneMarie Adcock, and cousins Kathee and Gary, Sara and Bryan.

I honorably acknowledge best selling author Adriana Trigiani for making this book publishing dream come true and to Emmett Towey of Project Main Street for supporting families fighting Lou Gehrig's disease and for all the great work Project Main Street does to support people with ALS.

To the exceptional companies I have had the honor of working for, including The Corporate Image - Jon & Lisa Lundberg, Jane Arthur, Robbie Phillips, Marty Engle, Mary

Herrera, Jill Oxendine, Esther Smith, Alyson Watson, Anthony Duncan, Ray Barnes, Deborah Smith; the Sprint family; the Bristol Herald Courier; and the Newport News Daily Press.

A sincere thank you to the ALS personnel from Tennessee, Virginia and the National organization, with special thanks to Cheri Sanders, Karen Bowdle, Brenda Hrivnak, Jane Luethke, Karen Duffy, Jennifer Mundy, Alex Kurth and Judy Taylor.

Thank you to Matt McGee and Marty Engle for their generous contributions in the development of my " Silver Linings" CD: and special gratitude to Richie Kennedy and Frank Amburn for their many musical contributions.

My life was blessed by countless good people, including Mark, Lynn, Benson, and Sarah Redman; Sabrina and David Wall; Robbie and Leanne Phillips and daughters Reagan and Ryann; David & Connie Wadsworth; Brent and Robin Kennedy; Trace and Becky Bratton; Mary and William Wampler; John Mack and the Pioneering Healthier Communities friends; Alice Loberg; Roman and Lynn Klein and family; Justin Malone; Donell Busroe; Wil Cantrell; Jeff Williams; Bob Ashley; Dale Cook; Mike Nidiffer; Mike and Jennifer Hamlin; LeAnn Hughes; Jerry "Santa" Rector; Brent Roswall; Jeff Harrison; Jim Daniels; Pam, Hal and Brad Cole; Ann Cunningham; Holly Nester; Virginia Tech basketball star Erick Green; Linda Stollings; Gloria & Sharon Phillips; Heather Smith and Rhonda Johnson; Bill Chaffin; Edwin Lacey; and Central Presbyterian friends, praise team band members and elders.

Lifelong friendships are appreciated through the love of: Shaun Levesque and Jim Wynne; Les and Annette McSpadden, daughter Katie and sons Nicholas and Jaime;

Chris Ayers and the Bristol YMCA friends and Board members; Pepper and Heather Choplin and daughter Deanna; Teresa Ornduff; Ray and Carolyn Jones; Pam, Lance and Luke Collie; John Stafford; and Jane Stikeleather.

A big thank you to friends of son Joseph and daughter Katie who have made visits, attended events, sent cards and shown their love to my family including, Jen and Rob Hull, Erica Schwartz and Noah Green, Cristina Fleury, Megan Ryan, Jeff Dimengo, Lauren Barnette and Matt Sanger, Maggie, Andrew and Amelia Holden, Cherith, Jason and Hayden Southworth, Amanda Cupp and Anthony Farnum, Brittany Jessee, Meghan and Scott Shaffer, Adam Rehberg, and Taylor Hensley.

To additional and important extended family members Alice and Howard Prince, Kim Prince, Jane and Bob West, Knoxville Princes Ty, Drew, Fran, and Karen, the late Thurman Musick, Gary and Rebecca Musick, Colleen and Jonathan Musick, Emily Musick, and Mark and Emily Musick.

To those who have been "silver linings" in the life of daughter Beth - Linda Stout, Nancy Brown and Peggy Dowdy; Brenda Vernon and her English challenge class; Justin Hale; Shannon Eldreth; Sherri Davidson Ginn; April Fletcher; Jan Black; Underwood Elementary 5th grade classmates; students and teachers at Athens Drive High School; Southeastern Rett Syndrome leader Marilyn Archibald; Abingdon High School; and those educators and therapists who had a positive impact in her life.

To the teams of medical experts who compassionately cared for the medical challenges facing me and my family, including Dr. Jonathan Glass and Emory ALS Center staff; Dr. Alan Percy, Jane Lane, and the Rett Syndrome family; Dr. Sean

Mullins; the late Dr. Roman Karpenic; Dr. Rick Whiles and Sapling Grove staff; and Dr. Jim Schrenker and Caris Hospice Group.

A heartfelt thank you to organizations that moved my life forward including, Service Dogs of Virginia and their wonderful staff led by executive director Peggy Law; The Atlanta Braves Organization including John Schurholz, pitching coach Roger McDowell, and players Dan Uggla, Paul Maholm, Jordan Schafer, Justin Upton, and Reed Johnson; Virginia Tech head baseball coach Pete Hughes; Virginia Tech Marching Virginians and Director David McKee; Bill Gatton Honda of Bristol; The Daniel Foundation; Bristol White Sox; Kingsport Mets; Knoxville Smokies; The Remedy Band led by Dr. Marty Prince; Country Club of Bristol; Wellmont Health System; Alpha Natural Resources; Crabtree Buick; Bristol Tennessee Essential Services; Bristol Virginia Utilities; and Machiavelli's Restaurant.

An extraordinary thanks for the gift of a handicap accessible van from Bobby and Courtney Kilgore.

I acknowledge and thank the hundreds of Facebook friends who have encouraged me to live in a strong and beautiful way through their messages of support. Thanks to every single contributor to Team Timp, the ALS Association, the Emory ALS Center and the Beth Foundation.

A special acknowledgement to the following churches and organizations to which I delivered "Silver Linings" and who contributed to our fight against ALS: Piney Flats United Methodist Church, Holy Trinity Lutheran Church, Thanksgiving Silver Lining at Southwest Virginia Museum, Greystone Baptist Church, Wise Kiwanis Club, 31 Club Banquet, Wise Baptist Church, Appalachian Prayer Fellowship

Church, Grace Fellowship Church, Bristol Rotary, United
Methodist Church Spring Banquet, One Enchanted Evening at
Bristol Mall, Bristol Kiwanis Club, West Hills Baptist Church,
Bristol Optimist Club, Avoca Christian Church, Speedway
Rotary, Wise Presbyterian Church, Pound Presbyterian
Church, Bristol Noon Rotary, Kingsport Sunshine Rotary,
Suburban Christian Church, Mary's Chapel, Beech Grove
United Methodist Church, Concordia Lutheran Church, First
United Methodist Church, Milligan College Occupational
Therapy Program, Jefferson College, Carson-Newman
University, King University, Victory Baptist, Range
Community Christian Church, Lebanon Memorial United
Methodist Church, Lebanon Recovery, Asheville Sober Living
Home, Tri-Cities Chapter Public Relations Society of America,
Elizabethton Rotary, Academy at King, First Baptist Church of
Honaker, Tennessee YMCA Executive Director Conference,
Saltville Baptist Church, Childcare Connections, State Street
United Methodist Church, First Baptist Church of Bristol,
Wise County Public Schools Special Education and Special
Services Departments, High Point Elementary School,
Lynchburg College AFP, Virginia High School, Applebee's
Restaurant of Bristol Tennessee.

## About ALS

Often referred to as Lou Gehrig's Disease, amyotrophic lateral sclerosis (ALS) is a progressive, fatal neuromuscular disease with no known cure that slowly robs the body of its ability to walk, speak, swallow and breathe. The life expectancy of an ALS patient averages 2 to 5 years from the time of diagnosis.

Every 90 minutes a person in this country is diagnosed with ALS and every 90 minutes another person will lose their battle against this disease. Based on U.S. population studies, a little over 5,600 people in the U.S. are diagnosed with ALS each year. Presently it costs loved ones an average of $200,000 a year to provide the care ALS patients need.

## Contributions

ALS was first described in 1869 by French neurologist Jean-Martin Charcot, but it wasn't until 1939 that Lou Gehrig brought national and international attention to the disease when he abruptly retired from baseball after being diagnosed with ALS. It is hard to believe that after 144 years there is still no known cause nor cure for this horrible disease; obviously, research to find a cure for ALS is highly underfunded.

If you are interested in making a difference in the lives of people with ALS and want to contribute to this cause, below are the significant organizations that helped Phillip Timp through his journey:

- Emory ALS Center Office: 101 Woodruff Circle, Suite 6000 Atlanta, GA 30322; contact.als@emory.edu

- The ALS Association Tennessee Chapter: PO Box 40244 Nashville, TN 37204-0244

- ALS Association - DC/MD/VA Chapter: 7507 Standish Place Rockville, MD 20855

If you are interested in helping the Timp's financially help families with children with rare or severe disabilities please contribute at:

- The Beth Foundation, Katie Timp, Executive Director; www.bethfoundation.org

If you are interested in supporting the important work of Service Dogs of Virginia, where Phil received his companion Nelson, please contribute at:

- Service Dogs of Virginia: PO Box 408 Charlottesville, VA 22902; info@servicedogsva.org

If you are interested in supporting Project Main Street, the group who financed this project and made this dream come true, please contribute and learn more about this wonderful organization at:
- http://www.projectmainst.org
- Project Main St.
244 Fifth Avenue Suite #2417
New York, NY 10001